Chinese Buddhism Today

Oxford Centre for Buddhist Studies Monographs
Series Editor: Richard Gombrich, Oxford Centre for Buddhist Studies

The Oxford Centre for Buddhist Studies promotes teaching and research into all Buddhist traditions, as found in texts and in societies, and is equally open to the study of Buddhism by methods associated with the humanities (philology, philosophy, history) and the social sciences (anthropology, sociology, politics). It insists only on using sources in their original languages and on aiming at the highest scholarly standards.

Published in the series from Equinox Publishing Ltd:

Buddhist Monks and the Politics of Lanka's Civil War: Ethnoreligious Nationalism of the Sinhala Saṅgha and Peacemaking in Sri Lanka, 1995–2010
Suren Raghavan

Dudjom Rinpoche's Vajrakīlaya Works: A Study in Authoring, Compiling, and Editing Texts in the Tibetan Revelatory Tradition
Cathy Cantwell (with a chapter by Robert Mayer)

How Buddhism Acquired a Soul on the Way to China
Jungnok Park

Sermon of One Hundred Days: Part One
Venerable Seongcheol
Edited by Linda Covill
Translated by Hwang Soon-Il

What the Buddha Thought
Richard Gombrich

Chinese Buddhism Today
Conservatism, Modernism, Syncretism and Enjoying Life on the Buddha's Light Mountain

Yu-Shuang Yao and Richard Gombrich

SHEFFIELD UK   BRISTOL CT

Published by Equinox Publishing Ltd.
UK: Office 415, The Workstation, 15 Paternoster Row, Sheffield,
       South Yorkshire S1 2BX
USA: ISD, 70 Enterprise Drive, Bristol, CT 06010

www.equinoxpub.com

First published 2022
© Yu-Shuang Yao and Richard Gombrich 2022

All rights reserved. No part of this publication may be reproduced or transmitted in any form or by any means, electronic or mechanical, including photocopying, recording or any information storage or retrieval system, without prior permission in writing from the publishers.

British Library Cataloguing-in-Publication Data
A catalogue record for this book is available from the British Library.

ISBN-13 978 1 80050 231 4   (hardback)
         978 1 80050 232 1   (paperback)
         978 1 80050 233 8   (ePDF)
         978 1 80050 256 7   (ePub)

Library of Congress Cataloging-in-Publication Data
Names: Yao, Yushuang, author. | Gombrich, Richard F. (Richard Francis), 1937- author.
Title: Chinese Buddhism today : conservatism, modernism, syncretism and enjoying life on the Buddha's light mountain / Yu-Shuang Yao and Richard Gombrich.
Description: Bristol : Equinox Publishing Ltd, 2022. | Series: Oxford centre for Buddhist studies monographs | Includes bibliographical references and index. | Summary: "Fo Guang Shan, "Buddha's Light Mountain", is a Buddhist movement founded in Taiwan in 1967 and led by the Ven Hsing Yun (b.1927), who had fled to Taiwan from mainland China in 1949. It stands in the Chinese tradition of Mahāyāna Buddhism and more specifically is a form of Buddhism which in English is usually referred to as "Humanistic Buddhism" or as "engaged Buddhism". As the sub-title of this book indicates, in order to make Buddhism widely attractive and relevant he has incorporated every influence available. Gifted with a benign personality, he has turned his seemingly boundless energy and prodigious versatility to creating an institution which presents Buddhism as potentially a source for benefitting society through making life enjoyable. This book hopes to convey the movement's ethos primarily by focusing on his views and activities"-- Provided by publisher.
Identifiers: LCCN 2022002511 (print) | LCCN 2022002512 (ebook) | ISBN 9781800502314 (hardback) | ISBN 9781800502321 (paperback) | ISBN 9781800502338 (pdf) | ISBN 9781800502567 (epub)
Subjects: LCSH: Buddhism--China--History--20th century. | Buddhism--China--History--21st century. | Mahayana Buddhism--China.
Classification: LCC BQ647 .Y36 2022 (print) | LCC BQ647 (ebook) | DDC 294.30951--dc23/eng/20220209
LC record available at https://lccn.loc.gov/2022002511
LC ebook record available at https://lccn.loc.gov/2022002512

Typeset by S.J.I. Services, New Delhi, India

We are grateful to the Ven. Hui Feng and the Ven. Hui Kai for their assistance, and dedicate this book to them.

CONTENTS

	Foreword by Eileen Barker	ix
	List of Figures	xiii
1	Preamble: Previous work	1
2	Introduction: Our title	12
3	Karma, death and ancestors	37
4	Hsing Yun's ethos and activities	54
5	FGS and education	70
6	Public ritual at FGS main monastery, Gaoxiong	84
7	Ritual as symphony	95
8	Fo Guang Shan's activities: Edification through spectacle and entertainment	110
9	Offshoots of FGS	115
	Bibliography	121
	Index	123

FOREWORD

Some twenty or more years ago, I was wandering along Margaret Street in London's Fitzrovia when, passing an imposing Victorian building, I spotted a discreet sign in what looked like Chinese script, underneath which was written 'London Fo Guang Shan Temple'. The door was open so I ventured in and was met by a friendly old man who pointed up the stairs. Slightly embarrassed, I climbed to the first floor, where I was greeted by two elderly ladies who spoke no English but chatted away to me with welcoming smiles and pressed some leaflets into my hands. They also indicated that I was welcome to return, pointing to a calendar to explain (I think) that someone speaking English would be there the following Wednesday. Alas, despite my intention to do so, I never returned.

However, several years later, while in Taiwan, I was taken to visit the magnificent Fo Guang Shan Temple and Buddha Memorial Center where I was to gaze in wonder at what I was told was the world's tallest bronze sitting Buddha statue presiding over a long pathway known as the Way to Buddhahood, on either side of which were eight Chinese pagodas, each seven storeys high. There were, I was told, well over a thousand Buddha statues within the complex. I did not count them, but had no difficulty in believing this and many of the other superlatives with which my enthusiastic guide peppered his commentary. This was a very different experience from that which I had visiting the modest little temple in London.

My curiosity about Fo Guang Shan was rekindled. I wanted to learn more about this new religion. I knew it had been founded in Taiwan by the Venerable Master Hsing Yun in Taiwan in 1967, but only managed to gather a very general and rather fragmented picture of what I learned was a prime example of Taiwan's new Humanist Buddhism.

I had first become aware of Taiwanese Humanistic Buddhism (although not by that name) when, several years earlier, I had come across an unpretentious storefront temple in Hong Kong, where I had picked up a couple of issues of *Tzu Chi: Buddhism in Action* and bought a book entitled *Master of Love and Mercy: Cheng Yen* (Taipei: Jing Si Publications, 1995), chiefly because I was fascinated by the photograph of the beautiful woman in a nun's robe on the cover. Several years later, in Taiwan, I was to visit a Tzu Chi monastery with a thriving vegetable and herb garden, an amazing and lucrative recycling centre, a television studio, an impressive university and a calm hospital in various locations throughout the island. Then I read Yu-Shuang Yao's book *Taiwan's Tzu Chi as Engaged Buddhism: Origins, Organization, Appeal and Social Impact* (Leiden: Brill, 2012). By now I needed no convincing that Master Cheng Yen was an exceptional person and that Tzu Chi was indeed 'engaged Buddhism'. By now, my limited understanding of Buddhism as a religion concerned primarily with individuals seeking enlightenment for themselves in the hereafter was clearly being challenged.

I was, therefore, both honoured and delighted when asked to write a short preface to a book on Fo Guang Shan and contemporary Chinese Buddhism. Written by the University of Oxford's distinguished scholar, Professor Richard Gombrich (an expert in Sanskrit, Pāli and Buddhist studies, and one of the world's foremost scholars of Theravāda Buddhism) together with Professor Yu-Shuang Yao (whose book on Tzu Chi I have already mentioned, and who currently teaches at the Fo Guang University in Yilin), I could think of no combination of authors who could better address the questions that had been accumulating in my mind about the new Taiwanese Humanistic Buddhism.

I have not been disappointed. The book is a bit unusual in that it does not follow the familiar pattern of a monograph on a particular religion. It does, however, tell us a considerable amount about Fo Guang Shan (FGS), literally translated as Buddha's Light Mountain, its origins, growth, beliefs and practices and how its founder-leader, Hsing Yun, had been influenced as a devoted student and follower of the innovative reformist Tai Xu, adopting the latter's motto: 'Never think of what Buddhism can do for you, only of what you can do for Buddhism'. But the book tells us much more. It contextualizes Humanistic Buddhism, both historically and synchronically, by comparing the original Theravāda Buddhism with the Chinese Mahāyāna Buddhism, the Hindu and Jain concepts of karma as an act or deed with the Buddhist concept of karma as intention, and, most particularly, the differences between a Buddhism that focuses on death and ancestor worship and one that focuses on this life, compassion and, most obviously in the case of FGS, joy and happiness. Unusually perhaps for an East Asian religion, women play a major role in both Tzu Chi and FGS. Obviously enough, Tzu Chi has a female Master, but leadership roles have been filled by men in FGS and its offshoots. This, the authors suspect, is the reason for some of the differences between the two movements.

None of this is in the abstract. Humanistic Buddhism is practical and dynamic. Master Cheng Yen is known to cut through philosophical musings and/or endless ritual, instructing her followers to 'Just do it!'. Master Hsing Yun has been responsible for insisting his monks and nuns are educated not merely in Buddhist texts and practice but also in science, maths and languages – and is providing education for lay people as well. He has established numerous temples and other buildings for promoting his kind of Buddhism. He has propagated Buddhist arts such as literature, painting and music. This, we learn, is a Buddhism that has been modernized without losing the traditional spirit of Buddhism. Furthermore, none of this has been solely for the edification of Hsing Yun's followers. He has ordained both men and women from other lineages; believing in interreligious harmony and co-existence, he has met with important personages throughout the world and engaged in interfaith activity (according to FGS's London website, he instructed that a Christian cross on the façade of the Temple should be preserved). But none of this is at the expense of Buddhism – far from it. FGS is an energetically proselytizing religion, but it is one that still respects and has compassion for all humans and, indeed, all living beings. Rituals are certainly followed, sometimes in elaborate detail, but there is a pragmatism to the rituals – they serve a purpose here, in this life as well as in the hereafter.

The book does, of course, tell us far, far more – but this the reader will discover for him or herself. Whether we are considering the extravagant, yet sensitive and perceptive FGS of Hsing Yun or the more sober but impressively productive Tzu Chi of Cheng Yen, suffice it to say that the authors present us with a wide-ranging, informed and sensitive picture of Humanistic Buddhism. I shall be returning to London's Margaret Street with the expectation that I shall be able to recognize and appreciate far more than I did on that first visit all those years ago.

Professor Eileen Barker

Figure 1: Most Ven. Hsing Yun and Richard Gombrich at the inauguration of the London branch of the FGS, February 1992

LIST OF FIGURES

Figure 1	Most Ven. Hsing Yun and Richard Gombrich at the inauguration of the London branch of the FGS, February 1992	xii
Figure 2	Prof. Yao with incumbent nun, Xi Lai Temple, Los Angeles, USA, 2018	5
Figure 3	Monastic lectures to pilgrims on a guided tour of the HQ, Gaoxiong, 25 December 2020	53
Figure 4	Group of pilgrims at Gaoxiong, 25 December 2018	68
Figure 5	Grand Master Hsing Yun tonsures a Western novice at FGS HQ, 2014	72
Figure 6	The two incumbent nuns give a sermon at Yongjing, a branch of BLIA	77
Figure 7	Opening of a Water and Land ritual, Kuala Lumpur, Malaysia, 11 February 2018	87
Figure 8	Carnival of All Deities, held at the HQ, Gaoxiong, 25 December 2018	111
Figure 9	'Master Hsing Yun and Master Hui Li with African Buddhist disciples'. Hsing Yun is seated in the front row, 4th from the spectator's right, wearing a rosary. The tall monk seated to his left is presumably Ven. Hui Li.	120

Chapter 1

PREAMBLE: PREVIOUS WORK

The trajectory of our research

A few years ago, our interest in the history and the sociology of Buddhism led us to undertake research that we hoped would in due course lead us better to understand a new religious movement which was (and remains) very conspicuous in our environment: Fo Guang Shan [佛光山] (FGS), 'Buddha's Light Mountain'. This movement was founded and was still being led by a monk from the Chinese mainland, Hsing Yun [星雲] (1927–), now known as the Most Venerable Master Hsing Yun.[1]

We wish to show how FGS is in the mainstream of Chinese Buddhism, while consciously also trying to bring that Buddhism up to date. This is all encapsulated in the career and ideas of Hsing Yun. Every religious movement of a certain size and duration is likely to share features and characteristics with previous movements that have arisen in the same culture, and we hope to have shown, both in our previous article[2] and in this book, that FGS has much in common with other forms of Chinese Buddhism that exist today.

However, we have been intrigued to find that FGS not only has a place in Chinese Buddhism which would allow an analyst to see it as being a kind of common denominator, but also as having taken a distinctive step further. We mentioned in section 4 of our article that FGS has branches

---

1 In Pingyin his name would be written Xingyun, but since he prefers to use the old (Wade Giles) transliteration, without diacritics, we follow his preference, and sometimes abbreviate it to HY.
2 Yu-Shuang Yao and Richard Gombrich, 'Christianity as model and analogue in the formation of the "Humanistic" Buddhism of Tài Xū and Hsīng Yún', *Buddhist Studies Review* 34.2 (2017): 205–237.

in most parts of the world, and through those branches it plays a part in the lives of many members of the Chinese diaspora. Beyond that, it also shares features with various modern religious movements which have grown out of traditions other than Buddhism.

To pursue this theme in any detail would make this book less like a monograph and more like an encyclopaedia. But an example may suffice to show what we are driving at. Ven. Hsing Yun organizes huge religious festivals at which, besides the Buddhist pantheon, deities from other religions than Buddhism are worshipped and given prominence. These deities include the Virgin Mary. FGS not only claims to represent Chinese Buddhism and Chinese traditional culture, but also to reflect and interact with other religious traditions both Buddhist and non-Buddhist, some from China and some from even further afield; it is prepared to include both non-Buddhist worshippers and non-Buddhist objects of worship. The spirit behind this inclusivity is not an aspiration to convert other religionists, but to broaden people's sympathies and awareness and thus promote religious tolerance. Even if it is not spelled out, this does cut both ways: in presenting itself as the friend of all, FGS is also suggesting that this very universality makes it uniquely wise and benign.

While Stuart Chandler's large book,[3] published in 2004, made an essential contribution by giving a general description of FGS Buddhism, we concentrate on features of the movement which he does not cover thoroughly, and highlight why we think it is so successful. Though there is no shortage of published material by and about Hsing Yun, on him and the FGS, most of that is in Chinese, and what can be learnt from publications in English is still quite inadequate – which is why we have chosen to present a lot of factual detail.

Chandler's book includes very little on Hsing Yun's teacher, Tai Xu [太虛] (1890–1947), whereas we think it is important to understand that Hsing Yun was inspired by him and can be read as continuing Tai Xu's project: to dramatically reform Buddhism by making it relevant to modern life.[4] Other contemporary movements in Taiwanese Buddhism have been going on somewhat similar paths, but not in so many ways or on such a grand scale as FGS. The only movement comparable to FGS

---

3 Stuart Chandler, *Establishing a Pure Land on Earth: The Foguang Buddhist Perspective on Modernization and Globalization* (Honolulu: University of Hawai'i Press, 2004).
4 This is a dominant theme in Yao and Gombrich, 'Christianity as model and analogue', especially parts 1 and 2, so we have not repeated ourselves here.

in terms of its success is Tzu Chi [慈濟], but we shall show (in Chapter 4) that that has followed a very different strategy, one which makes it clearly related to modern Japanese Buddhism, whereas FGS is firmly in the mainstream of Chinese tradition.

In his book *Democracy's Dharma: Religious Renaissance and Political Development in Taiwan*[5] Richard Madsen has a chapter on FGS, subtitled 'The Buddhist contribution to democratic civil religion'. It is amazing how much he has managed to convey in 34 pages: one could not ask for a more illuminating introduction to FGS. As the subtitles to book and chapter announce, the book's main focus is on 'how the Taiwan case makes us rethink standard liberal theories about the requirements of democracy'.[6] Since we could not equal, let alone improve on, his treatment of this intriguing topic, we have ourselves given it little space, because we find so many other interesting aspects to the story of FGS – an *embarras de richesses*. While we have not had the opportunity to do thorough fieldwork on any Buddhist temples on the mainland, what has been published so far does not suggest to us that any temple or movement there can claim to have been as successful as FGS in the last hundred years.

Having already published a book[7] and two articles[8] about Tzu Chi, we decided that we would try to write a book about FGS, both because a vast amount of information lay on our doorstep, as it were, and because a lot of that information seemed to be colourful and therefore memorable. The main reason for the latter feature obviously lay in the ebullient personality of Master Hsing Yun. One has to go no further than observing that in most of the world everyone who studies the Buddha's teaching has to learn that the Buddha's 'First Noble Truth' is that life is unsatisfactory (the relevant Pali word, *dukkha*, is often translated, albeit rather misleadingly, as 'suffering'), so that the goal of a Buddhist should be to avoid undergoing rebirth, whereas Hsing Yun rarely mentions this, but encourages his followers to enjoy life. This,

---

5 Richard Madsen, *Democracy's Dharma: Religious Renaissance and Political Development in Taiwan* (Berkeley: University of California Press, 2007).
6 Madsen, *Democracy's Dharma*, p. 132.
7 Yu-Shuang Yao, *Taiwan's Tzu Chi as Engaged Buddhism* (Leiden and Boston: Global Oriental, 2012).
8 Richard Gombrich and Yu-Shuang Yao, 'A radical Buddhism for modern Confucians: Tzu Chi in socio-historical perspective', *Buddhist Studies Review* 30.2 (November 2013): 237–59; Yu-Shuang Yao, 'Japanese influence on Buddhism in Taiwan', *Journal of the Oxford Centre for Buddhist Studies* 6 (2014): 141–56.

surely, is a new form of Buddhism which sets out to radically transform the religion's ethos.

As soon as we got down to work, however, we discovered that the enormous range of Hsing Yun's ambitions and accomplishments, to say nothing of his publications (all in Chinese and very few translated) means that one could easily fall into the trap of cataloguing them without finding a pattern or being able to locate them in a wider context. With so many diverse strands to weave into a single fabric, where were we to begin?

Tai Xu had left on record his reactions, both positive and negative, to Christianity – some of them highly original – so this offered a good starting point. There were also two issues that it seemed worthwhile to tease out: firstly, where we found similarities between Christianity and developments in Buddhism and FGS, whether these should be ascribed to direct influence (Christianity serving the Buddhists as a model) or were analogous developments that had arisen under similar circumstances; and secondly, to compare the roles played by Catholicism and Protestantism, both active in the relevant environment.[9]

In due course we followed up with two further articles. 'Fo Guang Shan seen through telescope and microscope',[10] as the title suggests, ventures a few generalizations about FGS (the telescope) and deals with the parts played in the rise of FGS by individuals besides Hsing Yun (the microscope), intending thereby to put on record some facts to which we could allude in future publications – and have used below.

Then we approached FGS from another angle, that of the great Max Weber. In 'Max Weber's work and the study of Buddhism today',[11] we left aside Max Weber's general interpretation of early Buddhism, which we consider to be virtually valueless, because it is based on the scanty and very faulty information that was available to him over a century ago, but we explained parts of his account of Buddhism that remain sociologically relevant to our theme – even though there are dangers, which we hope to have elucidated, of confusion through using terminology derived from Christianity. Thus, in this book we have

---

9 Yao and Gombrich, 'Christianity as model and analogue'. The chronological order of our publications does not mirror the order in which we wrote them.
10 Yu-Shuang Yao and Richard Gombrich, 'Fo Guang Shan seen through telescope and microscope', *Journal of the Oxford Centre for Buddhist Studies* 14 (2018): 128-55.
11 Richard Gombrich, 'Max Weber's work and the study of Buddhism today', *Max Weber Studies* 18.1 (January 2018): 1–21.

barely mentioned the important but somewhat technical subject of the Buddhist statuses and roles relevant to a full understanding of the organization of FGS. The main reason for this omission is that we feel we have dealt adequately with this topic in our previous publications, not only in the article on Weber, but also in parts 3 and 4 of our article 'Christianity as model and analogue'.[12]

The most basic status distinction in traditional Buddhism is that between the ordained (the Saṅgha) and the unordained (the laity). Since many modern Buddhist movements have weakened or even obliterated this distinction, unwary readers may well assume that it is weak in FGS, but that would be a serious error. In part 2 of 'Christianity as model and analogue' we wrote:

> In 1992 Hsing Yun founded and headed the Buddhist Light International Association (BLIA) [國際佛光會] (Guo Ji Fo Guang Hui) as a global extension of FGS for laity. (Before that, the laity had no formal organization.) By 2010 he had established branches in the five continents, over 260 branches in all. FGS and BLIA together may be referred to as Fo Guang Ren [佛光人] 'Fo Guang people' and their number is estimated at about 6 million worldwide.

Figure 2: Prof. Yao with incumbent nun, Xi Lai Temple, Los Angeles, USA, 2018

---

12 Yao and Gombrich, 'Christianity as model and analogue'.

Historical context

Though we (and of course many others) have given a brief account of the context in which Hsing Yun founded FGS – and shall say more about it in Chapter 4 – the reader may find it convenient to have a few facts set out here at the beginning of our account.

The radical monk Tai Xu had found the Buddhism which surrounded him in China dreary and moribund, preoccupied with rituals for the dead, and offering nothing to help or guide people living in the world outside monasteries. His many ideas and actions designed to reverse this decay are summarized in part 1 of our first article on FGS;[13] the cardinal principle is that it was the vocation of a Mahāyāna Buddhist – and of course the Chinese considered themselves Mahāyānists – to do good to others, finding their own spiritual benefit in benefitting society.

As a very young man, Hsing Yun had encountered Tai Xu; he had attended his lectures and read some of his publications. After the war, Tai Xu fled to Hong Kong, where he died in 1947. He labelled his teaching 'Buddhism for human life'; Chinese: *rén shēng fó jiào*. (Hsing Yun slightly changed the name, but that is unimportant.) In English it became known as 'Humanistic Buddhism'. Though that remains the name generally used in the Chinese context, in most of the rest of the world it is best known as 'engaged Buddhism', a term coined in 1967 by the world-famous Vietnamese Zen monk Thich Nhat Hạnh (1924–2022). Two other Taiwanese Buddhist movements contemporary with FGS, namely Tzu Chi and Dharma Drum, likewise claim to teach and practise 'Humanistic Buddhism'; all are innovative, but differ widely from each other.

In 1949 Hsing Yun arrived in Taiwan in the flood of about 2 million refugees led by the Nationalist Guo Min Dang [國民黨] (GMD) under General Jiang Jie Shi [Chiang Kai Shek] [蔣介石]. The latter escaped the mainland when the civil war that had been raging there for over a decade ended in the GMD's defeat by the Communists under Mao Ze Dong [毛澤東]. Though he arrived as an obscure and penniless young monk, and religious innovation was restricted by the martial law under which the GMD ruled Taiwan until 1987, Hsing Yun managed to take over a temple in Yilan (northeast Taiwan), to attract disciples, and by degrees to found a new Buddhist movement, which in 1967 acquired land on which it built its own premises in southern Taiwan. Hsing Yun's

---

13   Yao and Gombrich, 'Christianity as model and analogue'.

amazing energy, initiative and *savoir faire* have enabled him to create a seemingly never-ending series of events and institutions. The latter included universities, and at one of these, Fo Guang University in Yilan, one of us (Yao) has held (and holds) a full-time teaching position.

Comparing religions, particularly Buddhism

Everyone who has ever taught or attended a course on Buddhism in a non-Buddhist country is well aware that before long the participants in the course find that they cannot avoid discussing the question whether Buddhism can be called a religion at all. It seems to lack major features that are common to the other religions which one will learn about on a World Religions course. These features are prominent in Christianity, and if the course is taking place in a Christian country it is tempting to assume that Christianity is a typical religion, and Buddhism is not merely atypical but perhaps even to be understood as in some ways antithetical to Christianity.

To state this in a general way: to become a member of a religion the first requirement may be assent to certain beliefs; that is why many people, including believers, consider that a religion may also be called a 'faith'. This assumption is valid not only for Christianity but also for most of the other religions likely to figure on a World Religions course. While those religions teach that correct belief (orthodoxy) is the foundation of membership in their church, it is usually not enough: they are likely to add that this belief, if sincere, must entail certain kinds of behaviour (orthopraxy). These behaviours include both rituals and a vast range of actions which harm, benefit, or otherwise affect other living beings (real or imagined), especially other members of society.

As the student of World Religions broadens the scope of her studies, she will soon discover that in fact the majority of religions in the world make behaviour rather than belief the fundamental requirement for membership. This dovetails well with the fact that for most people in the world membership of a religion is acquired at birth, and one learns the basics as one grows up in a social environment. However, that is not the main point we are making here. What we are saying is that most of the world's religions can be better described as ways of life than as doctrines. They may well teach their followers doctrines, but the doctrines, and the texts and institutions which incorporate them, may be concerned with matters that outsiders do not consider religious, and they may fail to draw clear boundaries between insiders and outsiders; for both reasons one can argue about whether they should not be considered cultures rather than religions.

When one is trying to understand religions, this is important, because it means that in some religions who is and who is not a member is a clearcut matter, and in others it is not. In Christianity and Islam the issue can, in extreme circumstances, be boiled down to who can recite a statement of belief, a creed, and who cannot. The religions that have originated in India and China are of the opposite kind: they are ways of life, and though they do include beliefs, those beliefs are secondary in importance to general features of behaviour. In the case of India, one such general feature is a strong tendency to hierarchy (e.g. treating all human beings as inherently unequal), which characterizes the religions that share the label 'Hindu'; another is an ethos that attaches paramount importance to condemning hatred, aggression and violence in human behaviour. This insistence on non-violence (its Sanskrit name is *ahiṃsā*, literally 'lack of desire to harm') probably began in a specific religion, namely Jainism, in northeast India in about the sixth century BC, but also came to exert great influence on Hinduism and Buddhism.[14]

China, where Confucianism, Taoism and Buddhism have all flourished for much of recorded history, is a well-known example of fuzzy boundaries: someone may consider themselves or behave as a follower of one of these, or two of them, or even all three, and usually all possibilities are freely tolerated. The variation is usually guided by custom and context.

In religions where belief is primary, on the other hand, just as certain beliefs are prescribed, others are proscribed as 'heresy'. This tendency is strongest in monotheistic religions; Judaism, Christianity and Islam (to put them in chronological order) follow the rule 'Thou shalt have no God but me', and consequently plural membership is out of the question and may even incur the death penalty.[15] In Ceylon in the nineteenth century, itinerant British Christian missionaries were not grateful but scandalized when the incumbent of a village Buddhist

---

14 That a religion or a culture lays emphasis on a particular value does not guarantee that its adherents will act accordingly. One must never lose sight of the gulf between theory and practice.

15 In 1971, when East Pakistan seceded from West Pakistan and took the name Bangladesh, the invading West Pakistani troops would confront people and ask them to recite 'There is no God but Allah and Mohammed is His prophet', and those who failed were killed on the spot.

monastery invited them to preach in the monastery;[16] in their many publications the Christians had the arrogance to say that the monks were bad Buddhists because they permitted their parishioners to worship Hindu gods.

This brings us back to considering how a student of religion whose expectations of a religion are guided by a Christian environment can be helped to understand Buddhism. The God of the monotheistic religions is an omnipotent supernatural figure who exercises what we can call cosmic functions: he creates the world and brings it to an end; he also determines what happens to living beings (or at least to humans) after death. In polytheistic religions (such as forms of Hinduism) the cosmic functions may be distributed between more gods than one; but in any case, human individuals do not have the power to determine the outcomes. By contrast, in the Buddhism preached by the Buddha, in which 'salvation' consists in escaping from the cycle of rebirth, that result can only be achieved by each individual for themselves; the Buddha can and does give good guidance on how to do it, but cannot take over the reins from the struggling subject.

In a monotheism, ultimately power (which is conceptualized as agency) rests with the one God and all prayers for assistance must be directed to him or to those exceptional beings, such as the Virgin Mary and saints, to whom he has deputed his powers. The most frequent and obvious reason for doubting that Buddhism is a religion is that it denies the existence of any power that creates or puts an end to the world: the world has neither beginning nor end, or at least none that is discoverable, so that the search for them is a sheer waste of time. What happens to living beings when they die is another matter entirely (see Chapter 3).

While some religions, including Christianity, make a distinction between praying for worldly goods (such as health and wealth) and spiritual goods (such as virtue and rebirth in heaven),[17] God is always the ultimate arbiter who decides who gets what. He may decide whether to reward human effort – but he may also decide not to.

Contrast this with Buddhism. It is often helpful to ask of any religion or world view, 'Who controls what?' Buddhism, both in its earliest form

---

16 Kitsiri Malalgoda, *Buddhism in Sinhalese Society 1750–1900* (Berkeley: University of California Press, 1976), p. 212.
17 In Christianity these are called 'petitionary' and 'spiritual' prayer.

and in the conservative tradition known as Theravāda[18] ('the teaching of the elders'), strictly distinguishes what is worldly/mundane (in Pali: *lokika*) from what is supra-mundane, i.e., spiritual (in Pali: *lokottara*), but the difference from monotheism is even greater: ultimately power lies only with sentient individuals. This power, known as karma, is the very heart of Buddhist ideology.

However, less than half a millennium after the Buddha's death (we cannot be sure precisely when) there emerged a form of Buddhism, the Mahāyāna, in which benign supernatural figures play a crucial role which includes bringing their worshippers to salvation (= Enlightenment), in a way that allows one to describe that religion as a form of polytheism. In modern times this has been a focal point of controversy. The great scholar and ideologue Ven. Yin Shun [印順] (1906-2005) was the foremost advocate that Buddhism should 'participate actively in human society', and he decried 'worshipping Buddhas as though they were deities, a tendency that, in his opinion, has plagued the Mahayana tradition since its inception'.[19]

'Buddha' is a Pali title which literally means 'awoken', which refers to waking up to reality, the basic truths about life and the world. Already in the earliest texts, the Buddha, the person who gained Enlightenment and then taught it to others, is referred to before his Enlightenment by the Pali word *bodhisatta*, which in Sanskrit became *bodhisattva*, and came to refer to someone – normally a human being – who has made a vow to follow in the Buddha's footsteps, gain Enlightenment for themselves and help others to do likewise. The bodhisattva is a pivotal figure in all the many forms of Mahāyāna, though interpreted in different ways. One can however generalize by saying that it somewhat blurs the Buddha's distinction between the Buddha,[20] whose teaching and actions all concern the supra-mundane, and gods, whose sphere is unambiguously worldly. Devotees are urged themselves to become bodhisattvas, and bodhisattvas who have approached Buddhahood are available to help other beings with all their problems both worldly and spiritual.

---

18 This is widely used as a label for pre-Mahāyāna Buddhism; though this is not perfectly accurate, in our context it can serve as such.
19 Chandler, *Establishing a Pure Land on Earth*, p. 43.
20 In the Mahāyāna there are also many – sometimes infinitely many – Buddhas; they are not always individuated and in some cases there may be little difference between them and bodhisattvas.

The Mahāyāna teaches that the universe is infinite in every dimension, and it enveloped the cultures of most of eastern Asia. For both these reasons it is not surprising that in the two thousand years of its history it has developed many different doctrines and customs; no single volume could even adumbrate its variety. In that respect Fo Guang Shan is a child which takes after its parent. For the purpose of this book, however, we shall take as dominant two features: its internal variety, and its attention to the dead, particularly one's ancestors. The variety goes with polytheism, but in Chapter 3 we shall be looking at another aspect of its make up. Its attention to the dead is a salient but surprising feature, given that it claims to derive its inspiration from Tai Xu, who campaigned against this emphasis.

Chapter 2

INTRODUCTION: OUR TITLE

Chinese Buddhism: An unwieldy whole

The Buddha has taught us that every element of our experience is impermanent and liable to change. There is no reason why that should not apply to religions, even to Buddhism itself. Sociologists of religion have found that new religions are especially liable to change at the death of their founder(s). Though unfortunately our chronological information about the years following the Buddha's death is sadly inadequate, it is plausible that the major changes that led to the creation of Mahāyāna (some of which will be discussed in the next chapter) may have begun very soon after his death and the passing away of the founding generation.

Mahāyāna Buddhism has been in China for nearly two thousand years. In terms of both area and population, China is a huge country, and for much of its history it has been politically divided. It is therefore not surprising that its Buddhism has varied enormously both in ideology and in the practices of both institutions and individuals. Maybe the only common feature of Chinese Buddhism – and there are limits even to this – has been the institution of the Saṅgha, who have functioned to preserve and cultivate both texts and ritual traditions.

Chinese syncretism and superiority

Throughout its life in China, Buddhism has been seen as one of three great ideologies with their own concomitant values, institutions and practices; the other two are Confucianism and Taoism. These three systems have influenced each other, developing both similarities and contrasts. New traditions which are consciously syncretistic have also developed. The political authorities have not always been tolerant; but the overall picture is that the Chinese population taken as a whole have been prepared to study and respect all three systems. They have tended to be more prepared to accept that there is something called 'Chinese religion' or 'Chinese philosophy' or 'Chinese custom' than to take much interest in defining the differences between these large, vaguely delimited cultural entities.

Like all great civilizations, the Chinese have traditionally regarded their culture as the highest culture in the world. This has, we think, helped us to understand Hsing Yun and FGS; we return to this point at the end of this chapter. The variety within FGS soon brings syncretism to mind. On the other hand, those who study Buddhist movements naturally expect some homogeneity of belief and practice. Can syncretism and homogeneity be combined? Well, it appears that they can in China. This has led us to our title: we may find it paradoxical for Chinese Buddhism to see itself as a world religion – not merely as a rhetorical fancy or a missionary aspiration, but as a simple fact – but that is Hsing Yun's basic assumption, a truth which he aims to present with pride to the world around him.

Why has he been so successful? Inventions and discoveries in human culture which answer several disparate purposes are particularly likely to survive and flourish. Historians of Indian religion rightly point out that the most successful Hindu scripture of all time, the *Bhagavad Gītā*, contains incompatible teachings, but wrongly tend to find this paradoxical; on the contrary, it thus appeals to people with very diverse religious inclinations. Similarly, the survival of the Saṅgha for two and a half thousand years may well be because it has shown itself able to answer to so many purposes.

As we shall illustrate, a religion may be full of ambiguous and even incompatible teachings, even if we leave aside all the variations that are likely to evolve simply because of changes in time and place. A vast range of ambiguity may arise merely because the religion's exegetes wish to cater to followers who differ in their degree of sophistication; moreover, it is common for there to be disagreement about how literally teachings are to be taken and when we should understand statements to be intended as metaphorical. Thus, for example, two religious traditions may have common roots, from which they inherit the same sacred texts or ritual practices, and yet have developed quite contrasting characters.

Gnostic soteriologies

According to most Indian religious traditions, whether Buddhist or Hindu, subject and object are interdependent. As one advances towards enlightenment, or whatever the religion in question calls its goal, one's subjective experience of the world changes in a way not perceptible to the uninvolved bystander. In particular, the ultimate aim of religious practice for the individual is gnosis, 'realization' or 'understanding'. Gnosis is a technical term for the salvific awareness that one has in fact been enlightened all along, but simply has failed to realize that fact. Similarly, in Mahāyāna Buddhism the correct use of language, which abandons dualism, corresponds to the enlightened view of reality, but this does not mean that the normal use of language, which communicates between unenlightened people, is invalid or false: one can view it simply as expressing a lower form of truth, important in daily life. Believers in the Pure Land (of whom more below) can experience rebirth in it during their life in this world, and can truthfully talk about it, while at the same time sharing both experience of the workaday world and discourse about it with those who are spiritually less advanced. The experience is a spiritual state attainable only by perfect internal purity, and that in turn depends on unwavering devotion to Amida Buddha and steadfast concentration on his salvific agency.

Two major sects with contrasting soteriologies: Zen and Pure Land

Buddhism in China and Japan has over the centuries split into a number of separate traditions (of which the larger ones tend to be known as 'sects'). Some of them have died out. Two which have not merely survived but continued to flourish until today are Zen (=Chinese Ch'an) and Pure Land Buddhism. Japanese religious history contrasts with the Chinese, in that in Japan boundaries are clearly drawn in both theory and practice; both Zen and Pure Land, apparently antithetical, have split into several autonomous traditions. Nevertheless, in Japan the contrast between the two groups survives: Zen is held to be typical of *jiriki*, literally 'own power', meaning that one has to reach Enlightenment by one's own efforts (as the Buddha preached), while Pure Land Buddhism is typical of *tariki*, literally 'other power', according to which Enlightenment can only come through the help of a Mahāyānist Buddha called Amida (Sanskrit: Amitābha: Infinite Light). We shall see in this chapter how the Chinese, including Fo Guang Shan, have managed to syncretize even across this divide.

In China the two have often been combined. Describing the great Ch'an (=Jap. Zen) monasteries of central China in the 1930s, Holmes Welch writes that many monasteries had both a meditation hall and a hall for reciting the Buddha's name, though in some monasteries the same hall could be used for both. Every day monks sat all day in Ch'an meditation, which was their 'work'. There were perhaps eight periods of work a day, mostly of about an hour, and 'each period was divided into circumambulation and sitting. While the inmates circumambulated, they recited Buddha's name aloud'. While they sat, they either tried to solve a metaphysical riddle[1] (Jap. *koan*) or concentrated on the Buddha's name. Senior monks gave explanations 'of both Ch'an and Pure Land methods. Since both sects aim to reduce attachment to the ego, they saw no contradiction'. The abbot remarked to Welch: 'Who is going to help you stop your whole mind from stirring? You have to do it yourself. In Pure Land just as much as in Ch'an, you have to depend on yourself'.[2] One can call this syncretism, or a soteriology of 'belt and braces': if one form of practice does not satisfy, one is free to try something quite different – and need not even entirely abandon the first option.

This world a heaven?

Both Zen and Pure Land have contributed a great deal to the creation of Fo Guang Shan; nevertheless, it will give a clearer picture of Hsing Yun's place in the history of Buddhism if we begin at the other end, as it were, by recalling how they relate to the origin of the whole story: the Buddha's own teaching.

It is easy to forget that the Buddha's original message was predicated on what most people in the modern world, particularly in the West, regard as a decidedly negative picture of what life in this world has to offer. He and those around him believed that all of mankind (and the other creatures living in the world) were destined after death to be reborn, and though they believed that there were forms of life, notably

---

1 Not a good translation of *koan*. 'Paradoxical question' may come nearer.
2 Holmes Welch, *The Practice of Chinese Buddhism 1900-1950* (Cambridge, MA: Harvard University Press, 1967), pp. 398-99.

in various heavens, which were pleasant to experience, those were difficult to attain; moreover, even those lives (yes, even those spent in a heaven) were destined to end in death. Because every life led to the terrors of death, and involved a range of other sufferings physical and mental, not only was the average life not worth living, but the universe as a whole appeared as a kind of prison, and rebirth in it as a cycle from which there was no escape.

There were thinkers in India before the Buddha who had devised a doctrine that it was possible for a very few people, probably males born into the Brahmin caste, to acquire access to spiritual experiences which led after death to their merging into what we may call the soul or essence of the universe, from which they would never return. These religious virtuosi, as Max Weber would have called them, were however extremely few and most people were unlikely ever to meet one of them or benefit from his teachings, which were probably esoteric.

By the time of the Buddha, the fifth century BC, there were also a few other preachers, mostly itinerant, who claimed that if their disciples imitated their ascetic way of life, they too might escape rebirth. With hindsight we can consider that the most important of these was an ascetic known to his followers as Mahāvīra, 'Great Hero', and accorded the title of Jina, 'Conqueror', because he had conquered all his passions and desires. (The religion he founded, Jainism, is still centred in India and has something in the region of five million adherents spread around the world.) Not only did Mahāvīra believe that by eliminating his desires he had escaped rebirth; he also founded (or re-founded?) an institution: that sincere believers could best cultivate a life which would lead to escape from rebirth by joining a celibate order of ascetics with two wings, one for monks and one for nuns. He thus anticipated both the Buddha's soteriology[3] and the basic institution of Buddhism, the Saṅgha.

In what tradition holds to have been the Buddha's first sermon, 'Setting in Motion the Wheel of the Teaching' (the *Dhamma-cakka-ppavattana Sutta*), he summarized his message in a formulation to which he seems constantly to have returned. He made four points, the 'Noble Truths'. The first of them is expressed not even in so much as a single sentence but in one Pali word: *dukkha*. Argument about the ideal

---

3 The Jain idea of a being which had escaped rebirth was of a spirit which, though immaterial, had a location, namely the apex of the universe. This paradoxical view of the form taken by the dead is of course found in many religions.

English translation for so basic a concept as Buddhist *dukkha* is mostly misguided, because what is appropriate will depend on the context. On a broad view, *dukkha* means 'unsatisfactory', but that is often too vague or too feeble a term. If we look at the context in the first sermon, we see that the old-fashioned translation 'Life is suffering' does seem to convey what the Buddha meant. The stark word *dukkha* is followed by a colon, and then comes a list which begins with birth, and goes on to 'aging, sickness, death'; then 'connection with the unpleasant, separation from the pleasant'; and finally 'not to get what one wants'.

This statement is immediately followed by the second Noble Truth, which can be described as an expansion of this final phrase, so that *dukkha* appears to result from the frustration of one's desires (including the desire for life itself); and indeed the third Noble Truth is that the only solution is to have no desires. The fourth Noble Truth lays down the noble Eightfold Path, which is how to lead your life so as to reach Enlightenment (= Pali *nibbāna*) and thus escape rebirth. The path refers both to morality and to meditation – both of them forms of self-control.

Expansions in other texts show that the Buddha was not going so far as to say that we can never experience pleasure or satisfaction, only that they are short-lived. The ultimate reason why life is suffering is death. While the words translated above as 'pleasant' and 'unpleasant' have no gender and could refer to things in general, what the Buddha had in mind was primarily death, both our own and that of those we love. It is relevant to recall the high rate of infant mortality in that society.

The Buddhist tradition relates that what made the Buddha renounce lay life was his first confrontation, as a young adult, with old age, sickness and death; though he was a flourishing prince, he learnt that even power and wealth could not help him to avoid those misfortunes. The story of how this happened cannot be literally true, but as an allegory it captures the very core of what inspired his mission to save all living beings. This is just as true for the Mahāyāna as for the older tradition: the Buddha's preaching is the primary manifestation of his compassion, the aid he offers to help all of us escape from suffering as soon as we can. Because our lives give us constant experiences of this 'vale of sorrow', the overwhelming emphasis on the consolation conveyed to us by the Buddhas and their disciples reflects the problem that dominates our lives and it is their mission to help us to cope with. Moreover, the role that the awareness of death and the consequent need for consolation have played in Buddhism from the beginning make it easy to understand why these emphases have played such a role in Buddhist societies, and why reformers (e.g. Tai Xu) have had to struggle to de-emphasize them.

In the Pali Canon, the teaching of the four Noble Truths is not just one teaching of the Buddha's among many: it is presented in various contexts as paramount. A few instances will suffice to show this.

(1) In the *Mahā Parinibbāna Sutta*, which recounts the last weeks (and last sermons) of the Buddha's life, he tells the monks, 'It is because we have not awoken to and have not realised the four Noble Truths that you and I have travelled and repeatedly traversed this long journey … When they have been understood, the root of suffering is cut off … and there is no more becoming'.[4]

(2) In a repeated summary of what the Buddha preaches while making a new convert, after a brief general introduction he is said to proceed to what Ñāṇamoli and Bodhi translate as 'the teaching special to the Buddhas' (*buddhānaṃ sāmukkaṃsikā dhammadesanā*) (MN 1.380, 2).

(3) When the Buddha is asked whether he is omniscient, he denies that he is so in the sense in which that is normally understood, but explains that he is indeed so in that he has understood the four Noble Truths (MN 1.482, which repeats MN 1.348).

The Buddha's first sermon begins with another component of crucial importance. He declares that anyone who has renounced lay life (which means becoming a Buddhist monk or nun) should avoid two extremes: attachment to the desires of the senses, and ascetic practices – what Christians call mortification of the flesh. Hence Buddhism became known as 'the Middle Way', a tag applied in a variety of contexts. Both extremes are the object of the second Noble Truth. Asceticism, the Buddha saw, draws attention away from maintaining calm and focusing one's thoughts on seeing reality as it is, just as sensual desire is a preoccupation with material goods. In his own quest for Enlightenment he had nearly starved himself to death, but it had not helped him. His competitors, the Jains, practised similar austerities while starving, standing still for agonizingly long periods, and exposing themselves to the elements, and the Buddha made fun of them for hoping to avoid agonies in future lives by anticipating them here and now.[5]

---

4 *Dīgha Nikāya* II.90.
5 *Majjhima Nikāya* I.92-4.

How does meditation fit into this picture? In the Canon the Buddha teaches several kinds of meditation, and others were added later, so one cannot generalize about its aims. Painful meditation, as we have just seen in the Buddha's encounter with the Jains, was not encouraged; the non-Buddhist term for austerities, *tapas*, is little used, and when used by the Buddha refers to self-control: to morality, not meditation. However, meditation too has a lot to do with control, for example control of one's attention and emotions. Self-control produces calm, and calm is an important kind of pleasure, and thus reduces suffering; this can be taken so far that enlightenment can be described as bliss; but – as we shall show below – it would be misleading to describe this as a way of enjoying life in the sense advocated by Hsing Yun.

There is however one further feature of the Buddha's teaching which is relevant to recall here: the eschatology. The Buddha, so far as we can tell, probably had little or nothing to say about the remote past or distant future; he preached that our problems are urgent and we should not waste our precious time by speculating about cosmology. However, some statements attributed to him in the Canon may be authentic. He probably reasoned that neither the beginning nor the end of the world were knowable, and that the universe proceeds through vast cycles of time in which the world alternates between eras of moral decline and moral improvement. What could affect our destinies was that we were in an era of decline, in which Buddhism itself was gradually disappearing. In a word, a very pessimistic picture – and one quite alien to Master Hsing Yun's sunny temperament!

Hsing Yun has throughout a long life been an amazingly active and prodigiously productive religious leader, who has spoken and written such a vast variety of advice and opinions that any attempt to summarize his views or attitudes would be unable to confine itself to making statements to which no counter-examples could be found. As one would expect of any educated and intelligent Buddhist monk, Hsing Yun has often alluded both to the doctrine of finding the Middle Way between hedonism and asceticism, and to the negative view of life so succinctly expressed in the four Noble Truths, especially the first one; and he has certainly never repudiated either of these two fundamental teachings. Even so, the optimism – indeed, cheerfulness – expressed in the title of Chandler's book, *Establishing a Pure Land on Earth*, is surely the flavour which pervades the Grand Master's personality and career, and which every account of him or of the movement he has founded must be sure to convey.

Hsing Yun's pragmatic and yet utopian optimism

We have explained in a long article[6] that Tai Xu, who a century ago opened a new chapter in the history of Chinese Buddhism, was concerned above all to convert Buddhists to realize that Buddhism was intended to serve people *in this life*, so it was a serious mistake to engage in Buddhist activities or even to think about them only, or even mainly, in the context of death, funerals, and the veneration of one's ancestors. Buddhist ethics, he argued, meant involvement in society and interaction with one's fellow men, not spending hours in solitary meditation or undertaking private courses of asceticism. As Chandler writes, 'To follow in the footsteps of the Buddha, avers Master Hsing Yun, means simply to tread the middle path, neither succumbing to the temptations of desires nor stubbornly insisting on rigorous asceticism. One will not find at Fo Guang Shan such practices as sealed confinement, long-term vows of silence, or the use of one's own blood to copy sutras'.[7]

In the earlier years of his ministry Hsing Yun did not much encourage his devotees to meditate; 'he considered Pure Land recitation a more suitable means to attract lay followers, given their busy lives, relatively low education level, and scant understanding of the dharma. Clerics were dissuaded from spending too much time in the Chan hall, for to do so was regarded as contrary to the bodhisattva spirit of serving all beings, not just attending to one's own liberation'.[8] He moderated this attitude in the early 1990s, but 'remained emphatic that Chan must be integrated into everyday living'. He regarded Chan as 'more a way of seeing and acting in the world than a particular form of practice'. He adopted the Chan maxim that 'A day without work is a day without food', but radically broadened it, so that by 'work' he has taken it to refer not just to agriculture but to all forms of industriousness. Chandler quotes him as saying in a lecture: 'The most miserable person in this world is one who does not have any work; the greatest privation in life is the loneliness of boredom'.[9]

---

6 Yao and Gombrich, 'Christianity as model and analogue'.
7 Chandler, *Establishing a Pure Land on Earth*, p. 44.
8 Ibid., p. 45.
9 Ibid., p. 46.

It is interesting to compare the passage in the Pali Canon in which the Buddha criticizes Jain ascetics with the following words of Hsing Yun, which we have culled from the internet:[10]

> In FGS we do not encourage ascetic (*ku xing*) practices because they are so cold (*liang*), long and boring. Your body can be strengthened by physical labour, but that is not FGS's aim, because you end up with pain in your heart and body. We promote the middle way in physical practice: we eat when we feel the need, we sleep when we feel the need. That is happy practice (*le xing*). It is not necessary deliberately to avoid material wealth. Happy practice is a better method. In that way you become more willing to work for others and serve them better. You will make people like you. Creating their happiness also creates your own. That is a complete practice. Many people think being a Buddhist involves going into retreat, but that requires discipline and that in turn requires knowledge of Buddhism. Even in retreat we are disciplined in our sleep and exercise. I have been asked to take the precept not to eat after lunch, but it is all right to take noodles so long as they are in liquid form. In the old days when we had no electricity we went to bed at sunset, but now we can have a longer day and complete fasting after lunch may make us ill, so there is no need to feel guilty about eating in the evening. What matters is to maintain good health.

We shall return below to Hsing Yun's warmheartedness. First, however, we must say more about the great debt he evidently owes to the Pure Land tradition. In some ways his views in this area go back to Shinran and even further, but the linchpin is that we are already living in the Pure Land, and this apparent paradox he has inherited from Tai Xu.[11]

Reaching the Pure Land

Pure Land Buddhism – as it is generally known in English – has been one of the major Buddhist sects of China and Japan for the best part of a millennium. It is the largest sect in Japan to this day, and also sometimes known as Amidism, Amida (derived from Skt. Amitābha 'Of Infinite light') being the name of the Buddha who is chiefly worshipped.

---

10 Hsing Yun's views on enjoying life can be found on the internet in a set of a hundred articles on Saṅgha affairs. The following comes from the first lecture on his third theme, which is on esoteric practice.
11 Yao and Gombrich, 'Christianity as model and analogue', especially section 1.

The largest of the many branches of the sect consider their tradition, which they call *Jōdo shinshū*, 'True Sect of the Pure Land' to derive from the great saint Shinran (1173-1262). Chandler's title, *Establishing a Pure Land on Earth*, is ideal for a book about FGS, since it can refer to the goal of the individual adherent, to that of the movement as a whole, to a spiritual transformation, and to an event (or series of events) perceptible to anyone in the public world of today.

Amidism, in all its branches, is typical of the Japanese form of Buddhism known as *tariki*, literally 'other power', according to which Enlightenment can only come through the help of a Buddha (normally Amida); its predominant practice is the repetition of his name, which is done to thank him for his compassion. 'Obedience to the Buddhist commandments and the performance of good deeds are not necessary to attain deliverance; ... it is precisely the bad man who can be sure of being born into Amida's paradise'.[12]

To explain the apparent multiplicity of forms both of *Jōdo shinshū*, and of Hsing Yun's religious thought, we must refer back to our remarks on gnosticism early in this chapter. On the one hand, subject and object are interdependent. On the other hand, a religious doctrine can be intended as something to be taken literally, or metaphorically; usually the literal version is for the beginner, or the less sophisticated follower, while after making progress in spiritual understanding one graduates to the abstract, metaphorical interpretation of the same or similar wording.

Thus, initially the worshipper of Amida regards their goal as rebirth, after their death here on earth, in a paradise, which is presided over by Amida and situated somewhere in the remote West. (Hence it may be referred to as 'the Western Paradise'.[13]) In this heaven they spend a blissful existence listening to Amida's preaching, and ultimately attain Buddhahood, which means passing on into the inexpressible void in which there is no distinction between subject and object, and thus no dualism. In one of his late letters Shinran 'explains that Amida and the Pure Land lie in ourselves'.[14] This is a form of the cardinal doctrine of

---

12 Robert K. Heinemann, 'This world and the other power', in Heinz Bechert and Richard Gombrich (eds.), *The World of Buddhism* (London: Thames and Hudson, 1984), p. 224.
13 The furthest back that we can trace this paradise is to a pair of Sanskrit texts of about the third century AD, where it is called Sukhāvatī – a name that has nothing to do with the West.
14 Heinemann, 'This world and the other power', p. 224.

many gnostic religions: the salvific enlightenment is the realization that one has been enlightened all along. To the devotee the world at that point appears transformed, but to the onlooker the transformation looks to be undergone by the devotee.

For Hsing Yun, 'there is no need to await rebirth to experience the bliss of a pure land; one need only fully realise the ultimate sanctity of mind and, hence, of all reality'.[15] Thus the title of Chandler's book, as we have observed above, is fraught with deliberate ambiguity, for it refers both to this world which we inhabit and to all of us, the individuals within it: it 'assumes that optimal spiritual cultivation relies on purifying both external environment and internal intention'.[16] This parallelism may also be applied to degrees of purity: 'Those who achieve nirvana through Hīnayāna practices, for instance, have gained self-liberation and are freed from birth and death, but they have not attained the highest form of realization since their practice is too individualistic'.[17]

The Pure Land is imagined, and depicted in scripture, as a heaven, though it is not one of the heavens posited by early Buddhist cosmology. Those reborn in this heaven to join a perpetual Buddhist congregation have not quite attained Enlightenment or nirvana, but that final disappearance from the cosmos is guaranteed as their final destiny. There is a tradition of constructing a small-scale replica of the Pure Land inside the monastery. In some branches of the sect this has developed into the idea that those who are sufficiently pious can work this transformation of their monastic surroundings into a Pure Land – much as the pious disciple of some gnostic religions may achieve their goal by realizing that they have been enlightened all along.

According to Hsing Yun, even this world around us can be a serene pure land so long as the mind is tranquil; 'a tranquil mind transforms and purifies the surroundings. There is ... no need to await rebirth to experience the bliss of a pure land; one need only fully realize the ultimate sanctity of mind and, hence, of all reality'.[18]

At this juncture Hsing Yun has introduced the characteristic ethos of Humanistic Buddhism.

---

15 Chandler, *Establishing a Pure Land on Earth*, p. 47. In this context, sanctity and purity seem to be interchangeable metaphors.
16 Ibid.
17 Ibid.
18 Ibid.

24   *Chinese Buddhism Today*

> Because the purity of mind necessary for meditation and recitation depends on the satisfaction of certain basic material needs, attending to those needs for oneself and others is an ineluctable part of Buddhist practice. Master Hsing Yun does not want people passively to accept their present conditions while awaiting rebirth. He states: 'Today there are many Buddhists who wish to be reborn in the Sukhavati Pure Land, but I think that that is not as good as putting one's energies to changing today's world into a Buddhist pure land'. The Western Pure Land does not exist, but since for the time being we live in this world, this is where we should concentrate our energies.[19]

Here we encounter an important theme of FGS: the Master's view of Buddhism as enhancing life on earth. The world, he preaches, improves in every respect as it progresses through time. This extremely positive view of human history stands in startling contrast to early Buddhist eschatology (see above), and the exhortation to action similarly deviates from Shinran.

> [I]f several hundred years ago someone had suggested that roads could be paved so that they were smooth and clean or that a person living high up in a building could have running water, no one would have believed it, yet today such things are commonplace. We have air-conditioning in hot summers; automobiles, trains and airplanes that will take us to far-off places for work or recreation; delicious food; and radio and television broadcasts that can be heard around the world instantaneously. 'Truly, we can have whatever we want and do whatever we wish. Hence, on the material level this world of ours is gradually developing such that it is virtually indistinguishable from a heaven'.

Moreover, 'the global trend toward democracy and human rights also fosters the conditions of equality, brotherhood and peace required for cultivation. The notion of humanity's steady progress through history to ever-higher levels of comfort, freedom, ethical consciousness, and rationality is a central feature of the master's philosophy'.[20]

'The celebration of human dignity and potential has also been reflected in changes in religious worship. The honor once bestowed upon gods is now bestowed on those persons who have performed great feats. In other words, religion has been secularized to become a form of

---

19 Chandler, *Establishing a Pure Land on Earth*, p. 48. One could go on to argue that here one catches sight of Christian influence and the foundational work of Tai Xu.

20 Ibid. Though he has not much changed his tune, it is worth noting that this and similarly optimistic pronouncements date from 1983 and thereabouts.

hero worship'. This is no bad thing, 'for the shifting of emphasis from the supernatural to real people in our own world has rid humanity of much superstition and has caused people to take more responsibility for their actions ... and enjoy greater freedom than ever before'.[21]

According to Hsing Yun's version of the Pure Land cosmology, in the next and final era:

> [A]ll living beings will have an equal right to existence. People will extend their knowledge and expertise to benefit all living creatures. 'From the higher animals to the lower life forms, such as ants and insects, all show the same desire for survival and dread of death, all wish to escape pain and seek happiness. Hence, as the era of human rights progresses, we can certainly in the future enter into the era of "life power" that was promoted by the Buddha, when he said "All living beings have Buddha nature"'. ... There will be no need to pray for rebirth in a pure land, for the Lotus World itself will have been actualized. Dualisms of here and there, life and death, purity and impurity, will no longer apply.[22]

As Chandler concludes, '[T]he fundamental distinction between the early Pure Land school ... and other Chinese Buddhist philosophies is not the conceptual framework but the degree of confidence in humanity's ability to actualize the Buddhist experience effectively in the present age'.[23] Chandler shows how the struggle between these two interpretations of Pure Land soteriology has a long history; but what is important if one is to appreciate the flavour of Hsing Yun's Buddhism is how he manages to combine transcendent optimism with the ambiguity inherent in a gnostic creed, convincing devotees that they will deserve to live in a paradise, in either this or a future life, because under his guidance their own piety will have created it.

Advice on enhancing this life: American influence

When one first encounters FGS, one is overwhelmed by the way in which Hsing Yun encourages his followers to be aware of the pleasures that today's material culture has on offer and to take advantage of them. This is colourful material and we shall provide many examples later in this book. The positive ideology of the Pure Land tradition was

---

21 Ibid., p. 49.
22 Ibid., p. 50.
23 Ibid., p. 54.

presumably ingrained in him in his early years as a novice and young monk, but in Chapter 4 we shall show that in those years he had to sustain great hardship, and it is extraordinary that so many years of deprivation were turned into the soil which nurtured his enormous optimism.

Presumably the accelerating democratization of Taiwan in the 1970s and 1980s, the accompanying gradual takeover by American material culture, and finally the death of Jiang Jie Shi, came at just the right time for Hsing Yun to profit from them, even to exploit them, both materially and psychologically. It is obvious that the Master has been deeply impressed by American culture, not merely the universal emphasis on buying and selling both goods and entertainment, but particularly by the adoption of commercial habits by many Christian sects and movements of American origin. He has been wonderfully adept at mastering the use of modern technology (see Chapters 4, 6 and 8) and understanding its utility for gathering supporters and their donations.

Hsing Yun first visited the USA in 1978. In that year he founded a branch temple in Los Angeles; in 1988 that became Xi Lai, the largest Buddhist temple in America. In 1991 he attached a monastery to the temple and alongside it founded the University of the West. In 1989 he arranged for his mother to migrate from China to America. She lived there until her death in 1996.

Richard Madsen has written: 'Buddha's Light Mountain is not simply about reviving (and perhaps partly reinventing) traditional Buddhist ritual practices. It is also about publicizing those practices in ways that will teach and inspire people around the modern world'.[24] Madsen gives wonderfully vivid accounts of a chanting ceremony held in Gaoxiong and a public lecture given by Hsing Yun in Taipei, and shows how much the staging of these events has owed to American gospel preachers like Billy Graham. To use today's popular expression, the Master seized the opportunity to learn PR.

Hsing Yun urges his followers to get as much enjoyment as possible out of not only their lives, but also their Buddhism. This is an aspect of his 'Humanistic Buddhism'. We recall that he has followed Tai Xu in criticizing the general trend in most forms of Chinese Buddhism to resort to Buddhist practice mainly in the context of death and ancestor worship. But in our chapter on ritual we shall show that here

---

24 Madsen, *Democracy's Dharma*, p. 54.

too his version of Humanistic Buddhism is distinctive, in that while he encourages people to practise many death rituals, he at the same time wants those rituals to be occasions for making and enjoying music.

Get rich and don't apologize: enjoy it!

Many religions have preached that a virtuous person should not aim to be rich. For many centuries Christianity appealed to the poor (who are always in the majority) by stating that wealth on earth is not admirable and the poor will be recompensed for their poverty in heaven after their death. Only at the Reformation was this attitude to wealth partly reversed when Calvinists said that God allowed wealth to some as a reward for their piety. This became the ideological underpinning for American capitalism, and is still widely believed in the USA. Indeed, it may well be the influence that did most to form Hsing Yun's attitude to wealth.

Here is our translation of a magazine article he wrote in 1961.[25]

> In this issue there is an article by Sheng Yen [founder and Master of Dharma Drum] on whether the Saṅgha should own property. Let me respond. We respect Sheng Yen, who often contributes to this magazine, and focuses on Buddhist problems today, referring to the texts and giving his own frank opinions. Now he has written on wealth in the Saṅgha ....
>
> I think that nowadays our society has changed from being agricultural to being industrial. Money is the food which nourishes learning dharma and is the basis of Buddhist activities. The buildings and institutions we use to promote dharma cannot survive without money. Some think that poverty is how one shows one is a good Buddhist and they are afraid of being attacked for being rich, but ironically the same people go and beg money from others. Contemporary Buddhists need to change their views: there is no shame in being rich. It is poverty that is evil. We should not be jealous of the rich, or sarcastic. We hope that everyone will be rich: that will make Buddhism prosperous.
>
> Money is not totally poisonous like a snake. In the sutras it speaks of pure money (*jin cai*), kind money (*shan cai*), holy money (*sheng cai*). It is a thousand million times more meritorious to make good use of money than to pretend one is poor and learned. Amitābha

---

25 *Awakening*, 1 October 1961, reprinted as 'Everybody Rich' (*Da jia fa cia*) in Writings in Awakening, Collection on Buddhism 6 (Gaoxiong: Fo Guang Publications, 1982), pp. 48–50.

Buddha is in the ultimate happy land, and its floor is paved by gold, and balconies are decorated by 7 jewels. So why should the Saṅgha present themselves as poor? From now on, the Saṅgha should be self-sufficient. Apart from lecturing on the sutras and receiving offerings from devotees, they may try to take Sheng Yen's advice and run a farm or manage a company. If they have some savings, they need not be extravagant; don't make money by lending at high interest. At death Buddhism does not know where you have put your money, so lending it out would be a huge mistake.

Every country in the world wants to increase its GDP, so the Saṅgha should be rich (*fa cai*); that is the hope of the nation and the need of today's Buddhism.

This is an unusual line for a Buddhist leader to take. At the same time, Hsing Yun's praise of wealth does not imply any lack of compassion for the poor – far from it. He has always shown great compassion for the down and out, especially for orphans, and tried to help them, even taking them as his disciples.[26] It seems probable that in this regard he was deeply influenced by his own experience of extreme poverty in early life.

It would do Hsing Yun an injustice if we did not point out that he cleverly blends the capitalist view of being rich with his argument (which for all we know may be new to Buddhism) that one should not lend money at high interest. Though he does not use the term 'Middle Way', he does appear to be applying that concept. It has been said of him that though money has seemed continually to flow to him, he has so assiduously used it to support good causes that he has never actually possessed much. While outsiders have estimated that FGS is enormously rich, Hsing Yun has tended to give away money so fast – sometimes before it even reaches him – that he can at the same time maintain the image of the worthy mendicant.

The use of money by the ordained has been controversial throughout the history of Buddhist monachism. In early Buddhism, monks were not allowed to handle or possess any money at all, and their begging bowls were used only for daily collecting the food to maintain their lives. It is not untypical of Hsing Yun's innovations that his monks and nuns use their begging bowls as collection boxes.

---

26 We have interviewed two former monks whom he took in when they were in their teens because they were destitute, and a nun whom FGS adopted and sent to university when her parents could not support her.

Having fun

The Buddha was an infinitely kind and sympathetic person; even though he could be rather stern to individuals who stupidly misrepresented his teaching, he did not mete out any punishments or ever appear terrifying to his followers – a contrast to the God of most monotheisms. Nor was he a killjoy. But tradition makes him often repeat that life is inevitably sad and frustrating. Even the best human relationships end in sadness as all our lives end in death. Wanting any material goods tends to be a mistake, because the pleasures they afford are likewise finite. He is not recorded, we believe, as telling young people not to enjoy themselves; but he would have warned them not to waste the time available to them for learning to live calmly and wisely, acting for others at least as much as for themselves.

Unlike Hsing Yun, the Buddha never visited America, or had the chance to enjoy American entertainments; but most Buddhists in the world assume that they would have had little appeal for him. Hsing Yun has given much time and encouragement to sport, to the arts, to music and literature, and evidently enjoys them along with his followers. Under his auspices FGS runs a basketball team which competes at an international level; it is cheered on by supporters with cries of '*Oṃ mani padme huṃ*'.[27]

The gulf between sacred and secular in traditional Buddhist life[28]

The mainstream of Buddhist tradition, beginning with the Buddha himself, has in both theory and practice emphasized the separation between the monastery and the rest of the world: both production (economic activity) and reproduction (family life) are held to be the business of the latter alone. After all, the basic motivation for leaving home and joining the Saṅgha is supposed to be the wish to escape forever from this world, where life is permeated by suffering. Hsing Yun's insistence that people, including monastics, should enjoy their lives is at odds with the whole Buddhist tradition. His personal involvement

---

27 BLTV News, 6 March 2017.
28 This has nothing to do with the metaphysical distinction discussed earlier in this chapter.

with entertainments such as music, which most branches of Buddhism proscribe for monastics, and his use of radio and television, are part of this attitude.

The monastic tradition mostly discourages monks from acquiring education in secular subjects, whereas Hsing Yun holds the opposite view. When it comes to education in Buddhist subjects, the picture is somewhat confused. A large part of Tai Xu's life was devoted to making radical improvements in monastic education, which he regarded as the key to successful missionary activity, and Hsing Yun has been active in the same line, especially early in his career. When he acquired the means to build his own institution, he began by constructing not a monastery but a seminary; and his rules for promotion within his Saṅgha give more emphasis to educational qualifications than to anything else. His eagerness to found universities points in the same direction.

Despite all this, his attitude towards education remains unclear. It is essential to remember that he had a very deprived childhood and youth, which makes the accomplishments he displayed later in life all the more admirable. Nevertheless, it is notable that although in 1989 he arranged for his mother to emigrate to the USA and she lived there until her death in 1996,[29] and he naturally often visited her, and he also paid many other visits to English-speaking countries, he never learnt English. Similarly, he never learnt the form of Chinese native to Taiwan, namely Hokkien, and even for Mandarin he has often communicated through an interpreter.

When in 2013 FGS (which in effect means the Grand Master himself) established at Fo Guang University a Research Centre of Buddhist Studies and the Master came to open it, his short speech declared that research into Buddhism was not an important goal.[30] We can get an idea of what he means by this when one sees his frequent pronouncements that Buddhism is easy to understand, sometimes with an implication that one can learn as much as one needs from his own publications.[31]

---

29 We apologise that in our article 'Christianity as model and analogue', p. 215, we wrongly gave this date as 2006.
30 We owe this information to our late colleague, Prof. Stefano Zacchetti, who was present as an invited guest.
31 'A certain skepticism continues to color the attitude towards advanced scholarly research. ... [M]onastics who devote too much time to their own studies are seen as engaging in pedantic irrelevancies, losing touch with the concrete needs of common people'. Chandler, *Establishing a Pure Land on Earth*, p. 123.

We may venture to comment that this would not be the only case to be found in which a highly intelligent person will commend the benefits of education in general, and yet show scepticism about the educational standards actually attained.

When it comes to politics, the distinction between tradition and modernity follows a similar line. The traditional monastery tries to keep its distance from secular politics. Under favourable circumstances this may mean privileges: exemption from taxes or from civic duties such as military service. Some countries which honour Buddhism by giving heads of the clerical hierarchy offices of state have followed the ancient Indian pattern of a diarchy in which senior monks rule in partnership with kings and the aristocracy. On the other hand, for monks to take part in politics as individuals, standing for election and holding public office on the same terms as laymen (as now happens, for instance, in Sri Lanka) is a sure mark of modernity, and may draw the disapproval of more conservative Buddhists both clerical and lay.

In this area one may call Hsing Yun a modernist, because he has taken an active part in electoral politics, primarily because he wishes to ensure that the power of the state is exercised in a way that will benefit Buddhism. This however does not imply that he wishes the state to act in a way disadvantageous to non-Buddhists; nor has he ever tried, we believe, to draw the state into partisan politics within the Buddhist community. Chandler has a useful section 'Monastics in politics' (pp. 104-17), but that turns out to be about the Master's own activities; there is no suggestion that he has encouraged any of his monks or nuns to emulate him in this regard, and there are no political activists in the ranks of his Saṅgha. His own political activity Chandler summarizes thus:

> He is struggling to develop an appropriate strategy for giving his religious tradition a public voice. From time to time he has attempted to interject himself into the political process by endorsing candidates or participating in government-sponsored committees and conferences. His less direct solutions have been to cultivate close personal relationships with societal leaders and to lead high-profile public campaigns of moral regeneration.[32]

---

32 Ibid., p. 116.

Old and new

Perhaps the importance of the influence that American culture has exercised on Hsing Yun can best be conveyed by saying that he has adopted its message that modernity is *ipso facto* a good thing, so that any cultural innovation is to be emulated. The modern attitudes we have recorded have arrived from two opposite directions: mediaeval Japan and contemporary America. What makes them a complex and colourful mixture is that Hsing Yun contrives to preach modernism without sacrificing his allegiance to Chinese tradition: his syncretism often turns out to be a combination of the old and the new. Let us give some examples.

First, lines of transmission. In Chinese Buddhism these generally follow the same rules as does inheritance in a patrilineal society. There is more than one kind of teacher, but the most important is the monk who ordains you, who remains as it were your 'father' in Buddhism. The chronological order of a teacher's pupils is never forgotten and the father to son lineage may be maintained over centuries. Hsing Yun has made much of being Tai Xu's pupil, but he himself has repeatedly innovated, bestowing ordination on pupils, both male and female, from other temples. His most spectacular move was to let it be known that he was willing to ordain nuns from any lineage, going even beyond the confines of Chinese Buddhism. In 1988 he 'decided to offer the Chinese ordination rite to Theravāda as well as Tibetan nuns'.[33] The occasion he chose was the consecration of the Xi Lai monastery in Los Angeles. Two hundred and fifty candidates, male and female, from 16 countries were ordained.

He has changed how the hierarchy works in another way too. At the beginning of *The Practice of Chinese Buddhism 1900-1950*, Holmes Welch explains that in China there used to be two kinds of Buddhist temple, the

---

33 Sarah Levine and David N. Gellner, *Rebuilding Buddhism: The Theravada Movement in Twentieth-Century Nepal* (Cambridge, MA and London: Harvard University Press, 2005), p. 184. Since their chapter has many details of Hsing Yun's ordination of women, and these are not relevant to our main theme, we refrain from discussing this further here. They write that in 1988 Hsing Yun's purpose was for the nuns he ordained to 'establish Fó Guāng Shān ordination lineages in their own countries, thereby extending his own influence, as well as that of his order' (p. 184). However, the Ven. Hui Feng objects, citing his own conversations with Hsing Yun, that there is no such thing as an FGS ordination lineage, and Hsing Yun's sole intention has been to support women's ordination (personal communication).

public (*shi fang cong lin*) and the hereditary (*zi sun miao*). 'The essential characteristic of the hereditary temple was private ownership. It belonged personally to a monk or group of monks, who operated it as they pleased. On the other hand, the public monastery was supposed to be the property of the whole Buddhist Saṅgha and to be operated in accordance with a common monastic rule'.[34] FGS is a private temple owned by Hsing Yun, but he has given it features otherwise found only in public temples; the most important is that a member of the Saṅgha is not admitted (ordained) into the lineage of a current monastic individual but acquires the whole ordaining generation as his/her collective master. We believe this hybridity of temple type to be unique.

However, some of his organizational principles are strikingly conservative. Hsing Yun, a male, heads a Saṅgha which consists of 80 to 90 per cent women, and we have documented in an earlier article[35] that most of his early followers, starting from his days in Yilan, were women, and he had to depend on women to take almost all the important roles. This looks like a powerful blow for modernistic reform. And yet, though the leadership of FGS has changed several times, the top position has never been offered to a woman. Even today, except for a couple of comparatively large temples, the branch temples contain only nuns.[36]

Warm-heartedness and pragmatic adaptability

It would thus appear that the two most fundamental factors in formulating the positions that Hsing Yun has taken in finding answers to the innumerable problems posed by his extremely complex life and situation are features of his personality which a westerner would connect at least as much to the heart as to the head.[37] His treatment of women seems best explained by reference to the first. The most important feature of Buddhism, as a sensitive and perceptive person like Hsing Yun is bound to understand it, is its ethos of compassion – compassion for all living beings, but particularly for those who need it most: women and children, the sick and the aged; in a word, the disadvantaged. It is

---

34 Welch, *The Practice of Chinese Buddhism*, p. 4.
35 Yao and Gombrich, 'Telescope and microscope', pp. 128–55.
36 We owe the information in the last sentence to the Ven. Hui Feng.
37 Mahāyāna Buddhism offers a close parallel: the two most important perfections are compassion (Skt: *karuṇā*) – cf. heart, and understanding (Skt: *prajñā*) – cf. head.

this principle, rather than any theoretical argument, which determines how he acts towards them.

Pragmatism was a cardinal feature of the Buddha's teaching, and permeated his ethics. In the canonical *Vinaya*, the account of how and why he laid down rules for the community he founded, we can see how he adapted his decisions to circumstance; and in the teachings he gave to the laity we see how that adaptability shaped the ethical principles which underlay the whole edifice. The most basic building block of all was the law of karma. This must now be explained.

The Buddha had many ideas of great and perhaps disconcerting originality, and it seems that he had to employ what came to be known as his 'skill in means' to make them more palatable to his audiences. His central teaching about karma illustrates one of his tactics: restating a doctrine familiar from older local traditions but changing the meaning he attaches to crucial terms so as to subvert the doctrine's earlier meaning. Thus, *karma* originally simply meant 'act' or 'deed', and in a religious context meant an act that has consequences; by saying that he took the word to refer to 'intention', the Buddha created a whole new ethics and gave a new value to the basic fact of being a sentient being.

Thus, when a Buddhist makes a moral decision they cannot rely entirely on what a teacher (even the Buddha!) has told them, but must take account of the entire current situation. One effect of this is that there is no general principle that a rule must be (or must not be) taken literally: one first has to decide whether circumstances would make a literal interpretation inapplicable.

The karma doctrine teaches uncompromising individualism: each individual is a moral agent and is responsible for their own destiny. In the *Vinaya* the Buddha provided rules for monastics to follow, but ultimately whether and how they followed them was up to them. Outside the framework of the institution he founded, the Saṅgha, the Buddha provided moral principles rather than precise rules, and individuals were to consult their own judgments and consciences – though if they were sensible they would heed his advice.

In a series of articles[38] Dr Tzu-Lung Chiu has documented varieties of *Vinaya* observance among Buddhist nuns both in Taiwan and on the Chinese mainland. Thanks to her research, a good example lies to hand.

There is an ancient and still operative rule which forbids a monk or nun to handle money. Dr Chiu has found that FGS nuns are still

---

38 Most of them are published in the *Journal of the Oxford Centre for Buddhist Studies*.

following the principle that what matters is not the literal rule but the intention with which one acts. She writes[39] of an FGS informant:

> The nun ... does not consider that she has transgressed the precept against handling money, because she does so under the countervailing, and seemingly broader, ideal of being a bodhisattva. It is worth noting that the practice of benefiting others through the use of money is stressed by [Hsing Yun], ... who claimed that 'only a person who has a carefree attitude toward money and who knows how to spend it on Buddhism and the general public, truly knows how to use money'.[40]

Putting the unwieldy whole to use

In his message to Taiwan and the world, Hsing Yun deliberately blurs the boundary between Buddhism and the rest of the world. We have argued in section 4 of our article 'Christianity as model and analogue' that the content of what is offered by FGS in its many overseas branches is not simply Chinese Buddhism but traditional Chinese culture in forms readily recognizable to any Chinese person who is happy to be conscious of their roots, and the same message almost screams at the hordes of visitors to the Buddha Museum which has been constructed at vast expense (surely balanced by vast income) just outside the entrance to the Gaoxiong Temple, the movement's HQ. Again, Richard Madsen has perhaps been the first scholar from abroad to find the right words to describe this:

'Hsing Yun once said in an FGS promotional video that FGS is like a "department store that sells many things"'.[41] (We strongly suspect that, while making a serious point, HY was also exercising his lively sense of humour.) Picking up this theme, Madsen has written:

> Buddha's Light Mountain also intends to unify the eight major lineages of Chinese Buddhism. Almost any kind of Buddhist practice can be engaged in at the temple ... Since most people in Taiwan engage in some form of Buddhist practice at some phase of their lives, the complex of symbols offered by [FGS] contains something that can

---

39 Tzu-Lung Chiu, 'Rethinking the precept of not taking money in contemporary Taiwanese and mainland Chinese Buddhist nunneries', *Journal of Buddhist Ethics* 21 (2014), pp. 1–56. See p. 27.
40 Chandler, *Establishing a Pure Land on Earth*, p. 172. This footnote is re-copied from Chiu's article. Chandler here has further valuable information on this topic.
41 Quoted by Madsen, *Democracy's Dharma*, p. 58.

speak to almost everyone. Its symbolic net is wide enough ... even to include non-believers.

No wonder, then, that Madsen can quote an FGS nun as telling him: "'This isn't a religion, it is our cultural tradition'".[42]

Taking an even broader view, one can see that this matches a culture in which orthopraxy has priority over orthodoxy. Is this a matter of pragmatic heterogeneity, or a profound introduction to ultimate truth? Taking a truly Mahāyānist view, we can conclude that 'dualisms no longer apply' and secularity is just an illusion.

---

42 Ibid.

Chapter 3

KARMA, DEATH AND ANCESTORS

Issues concerning death and ancestors go to the very heart of Buddhism and impinge on many facets of its history.

As his reform movement's very title reminds us, Tai Xu can be said to have taken as his point of departure his harsh criticism of contemporary Chinese Buddhism for devoting far too much attention to rituals for the dead and the income derived from performing those rituals, at the cost of doing the many things which would directly benefit the living: he took the practice of charity by Christian churches as his model. As we shall show in Chapter 7, his pupil Hsing Yun has advocated simpler and cheaper funerals, but on the other hand has evidently taken pride in promoting many lengthy and often spectacular services such as the Water and Land service, the Obon, and the penance of the Emperor Liang, all of which are intended to make merit for the dead, both for the dead in general and for the late relatives of the congregation in particular.[1]

Buddhists believe in rebirth for all sentient beings. The cycle of death and rebirth goes on forever. Its beginning is a mystery; only the enlightened can recall their former births. The only escape from the cycle is to attain Enlightenment, which is also called nirvana.[2] Rebirth takes place in one of many destinies: heavens above our human world, hells beneath it, in this world as a human or an animal or a ghost (see below).

In the Buddha's day there were in his society two widespread beliefs about the fate of the dead. One was that the dead require regular recognition and worship from their direct descendants, and will repay

---

1 For more detail on these particular ceremonies, see n. 5 of Chapter 6.
2 The original metaphor behind Sanskrit *nirvāṇa* and Pali *nibbāna* is the 'extinction' of a fire, in this case the fires of passion, hate and delusion.

them by acting as guardian deities. The other was the theory which can be referred to as *karma*. Both of these theories and their attendant practices remain important today in every traditional Buddhist society.

Ancestor worship

Both in India and in China, the two main cultures which contain many Buddhists, most of the population is patrilineal, so that social identity is determined by the males. Sons, particularly eldest sons, dominate funeral rites, as they do most features of family life, and are responsible for maintaining the rituals they inherit. The entire emphasis of the tradition is not on explanatory theories but on ritual performance, which tends to be prescribed in minute detail and is often supervised by a priest. Initially, at death all follow the same course, starting where they died, though after a while they may move on to a heaven or a hell; ethical considerations enter only at the point where there is such a bifurcation. What happens to women when they die is considered very little or not at all.

Karma

All Indian religions believe in something they call karma, which they regard as a very important aspect of human life; but they interpret the concept in different ways, and this leads to much confusion. It suffices here to say that karma was important in brahminical Hinduism (also known as brahminism), and also in Jainism, before the Buddha came along and gave the term his own interpretation. Wherever Buddhism spread, the idea of karma spread with it, but its interpretation varied. The Buddha had many ideas of great and perhaps disconcerting originality, and he often employed the tactic of taking a term already familiar in the culture into which he was born, but changing that term's meaning. His use of this tactic makes it easy to understand how it came about that later generations disagreed about what he had meant. Luckily, however, if we understand the tactic it helps us to trace the development of Buddhist doctrine and practice (as we aim to do in this chapter).

The Sanskrit word *karma/karman*[3] originally simply meant 'act' or 'deed', and in a religious context meant an act that has consequences; a *karma* is thus likely to be observable, maybe even public. The Buddha declared, 'By *karma* I mean *intention*'.[4] This move is so audacious that one could compare it logically to saying 'By light I mean dark', or 'By fat I mean thin'. This move amounts to the claim that what really matters in life is not what one does overtly but what one *intends* by one's actions.

In a sense this turns the world upside down. An intention is something abstract, and if one wants to describe the quality of an intention one will use further abstractions; a pair of abstractions which is likely to be appropriate is an ethical valuation: intentions are thus readily categorized as good or bad, or as benign or malign. Actions can be categorized in the same way, but that is secondary: an action is good or bad because of the intention behind it. The moral quality of an intention generally does not depend on the nature of the intender: the ethical value of an intention is not affected by whether the intender is male or female, young or old, rich or poor – or indeed human or non-human. The concept of intention is thus fundamental to any ethical view of life.

Intention resides inside the individual – whether we say in the heart or in the mind makes no difference. Thus the doctrine of karma teaches that each individual is *responsible* for their own ethical decisions.[5] This is true whether or not one is obeying a command, because one is inevitably making a decision whether to obey that command. Similarly, one has to decide whether a rule is to be taken literally or not. This is why in early Buddhism no one, not even a Buddha, can save another being: everyone has to save themselves. It also means that the Buddha was perhaps the first to assert that all sentient beings are morally equal – until their moral performance renders them unequal.

Since all sentient beings, except for the very few who attain nirvana, will when they die in this world be reborn somewhere in the universe, it is natural to ask what determines where this rebirth will take place. In a general, imprecise way the answer to this question is supplied by

---

3 The Pali form is *kamma*. However, we use the word as it is naturalized in English.
4 *Aṅguttara Nikāya* iii.415.
5 Among Mahāyāna Buddhists, e.g. in China, it is widely believed that a group of people may together perform a karmic act and thus be reborn with what they call 'collective karma'. This doctrine is not found in early Buddhism and would indeed undermine the original teaching. See the Appendix to this chapter.

the doctrine of karma. One's destiny at death is determined by one's moral record. That record is not just a record of one's morality in this life, but stretches back into the infinite past; however, people rarely think of that, because it is only one's record in the present life that one is now in a position to affect.

It is perhaps easier to understand the karma theory if one realizes that its basic metaphor is agricultural: planting a seed and reaping a harvest. In popular usage karma is understood, confusingly, to refer not to an action but to the *results* of an action (in Sanskrit: *karma-vipāka* – *vipāka* means 'maturation'); as a result, when a lay Buddhist has a stroke of bad luck they may say, 'This is my karma', meaning that it must be the result of some bad thing I did (or rather, intended) in a former life.

The idea that the form in which one is reborn depends on one's record as a moral agent appears in Vedic literature in the earliest *Upaniṣads* (notably the *Bṛhad-āraṇyaka*), in Jainism and in Buddhism. Though it has so far not been possible to date these three texts with any precision, the first two seem to be dated a little earlier than Buddhism, since the Buddha responds to some of their teachings (without naming his sources). Obeyesekere calls this 'ethicizing' rebirth – which in both Jainism and Buddhism leads to ethicizing the universe. At first the basic model remains simple. This world is the arena of action, the other world is the arena of pay-off (*karma-vipāka*). When the pay-off is complete, you come back to this world and start again. However, what comes to characterize all the Indian soteriologies – Brahminical/Hindu, Jain and Buddhist – is that they add to rebirth the idea that by certain means one can escape from the cycle, and it is such an escape, 'liberation', that constitutes salvation. As Obeyesekere writes: 'There can no longer be a single place [after death] for those who have done good and those who have done bad. The other world must minimally split into two, a world of retribution ('hell') and a world of reward ('heaven')'.[6] All the traditions mentioned come to agree that since all lives are finite and a good rebirth will inevitably come to an end, the best solution – the only final one – is liberation.

In cosmology Hindus keep the underlying binary model: it is humans and the higher animals who are the moral agents, and at death they

---

6 Gananath Obeyesekere, *Imagining Karma: Ethical Transformation in Amerindian, Buddhist, and Greek Rebirth* (Berkeley: University of California Press, 2002), p. 79.

go to a heaven or a hell to be rewarded or punished. Though escaping rebirth is seen as ultimately the best destiny, most people aim for a good rebirth in heaven or in a good station on earth – and ethnography suggests that despite their different 'official' doctrines, very many Jains and Buddhists share that attitude, which leads to much inconsistency.

The Buddha's turning the earlier meaning of karma as an enjoined ritual act on its head entailed regarding ritual *per se* to be ethically neutral: performing ritual has no bearing on anyone's future destiny, and from the religious point of view is simply a waste of time. A good – i.e., a well-intentioned – act will bring good results for its agent; a malign act will sooner or later bring the agent bad consequences. These bad consequences look like punishment, but that view is not quite right, in that there is no punisher: it is a law of nature that the punishment will arrive, and who or what delivers it is not pre-determined.

In the Buddha's teaching, one may regret an action, but strictly speaking there is no such thing as atonement. If I do something wicked, I shall suffer for it: my bad karma has sown a seed which I shall harvest. But the situation is not as desperate for the wicked as this may seem, because although one cannot expunge bad karma, one can counterbalance it by performing good karma. Notwithstanding the Buddha's devaluation of ritual, the ceremonies performed by Chinese Buddhists, mentioned at the beginning of this chapter and discussed in Chapter 7, which in English are often called 'penances', perform that function: as will be explained below, by the virtuous intention of wishing to 'transfer' to the dead (typically to one's dead ancestors) the merit one is gathering, one creates for oneself good karma which one hopes will outweigh at least a part of one's own bad karma.

The Buddha denied that individuals have anything corresponding to what we call a 'self' (Skt: *ātman*; Pali: *attā*). Unfortunately, this has often been taken to mean that he denied personal continuity – a misunderstanding which could hardly be more extreme. He saw our lives as consisting of various continuities, both physical and mental; continuity means that each stage helps to determine the next one. The most important continuity is ethical, the continuity of moral intention – that is, of karma. As the British proverb says, 'Sow an act, reap a habit; sow a habit, reap a character; sow a character, reap a destiny'.[7] Karmic continuity lasts not only within one life but through an infinite sequence

---

7 Richard Gombrich, *What the Buddha Thought* (Sheffield: Equinox, 2009), p. 13; see pp. 7–15 for a fuller explanation.

of births, until the sowing ceases with the attainment of nirvana: the extinction of passion, hatred and delusion. For Buddhists, each of us has a biography which is in essence simply a chronicle of our record as an ethical agent, a record which extends over innumerable lives.

We have seen that Buddhists believe that rebirth may occur anywhere in the universe and in any animate form. At the same time everyone in traditional Buddhist societies is familiar with beliefs and practices, many of them obligatory, which put them in touch with the recently dead members of their own families. How do they combine these two very dissimilar theories?

For Hindus, it is in general impossible to alter one's place in the world after death, and therefore one's future enjoyment or suffering, because that existence is only for pay-off; they do not believe that those born in a heaven can continue to do good. In post-Vedic texts, the general picture is 'that sins, when not expiated by penances or by State punishment, lead to hell, and then, owing to some remnants of the evil deeds, to birth as lower animals, and then as decrepit or diseased human beings'.[8]

Buddhists, by contrast, have always gone to the extreme of ethicizing the entire universe. According to Buddhism, all sentient beings, however situated, from gods at the top, down through human beings, animals, ghosts, and ultimately even those suffering in hell, are part of one moral community capable of good and bad moral intentions which will inevitably affect the character of their future rebirths. In this they resemble human society, including all castes and both genders. This follows from the Buddha's radical position that *karma* is created by intention, which in turn means that any individual's moral standing, which could be said to be the most important thing about them, has no connection with any physical feature but is entirely due to what goes on, invisibly, in their heads. Thus any sentient being, whether human, animal, god or ghost, continues to have moral responsibility, and can, for example, be influenced by preaching (see below).

---

8 P. V. Kane, *History of Dharmaśāstra* IV (Poona: Bhandarkar Oriental Research Institute, 1953), p. 154. In quoting this great work, we have often taken the liberty of improving the punctuation.

The immediate fate of the dead

The Brahmin/Hindu view, which provides a framework for all their mortuary rituals, is that the dead person (initially referred to as the *preta*[9]) goes through three phases. The first, which follows death immediately, is very like what popular belief in the West has tended to think of as a ghost. It is in this form that the dead person inspires most fear and/or disgust. On the anniversary of the death there is a crucially important ceremony called a *śrāddha*, which marks stage two, the point at which the dead man joins his ancestors and moves from being a *preta* to being a *pitṛ*.

> By dying, the man left your kin group, and now you have restored him to it by making him an ancestor. The mourners' picture of the ghost in the period leading up to his change of status is extremely fluid. It is thought to inhabit a body provided by the mourners, yet it is also a disembodied spirit and may also be present in a person or animal. This diversity of form provides the relatives with the opportunity to feed the ghost through several different channels, thus minimizing the risk of failure and providing them with greater peace of mind.[10]

How was the Brahmin ritual adapted to a Buddhist context? A modern Westerner who accepts the Buddha's teachings on karma can see no logical reason why one of the kinds of being among which one may be reborn is a 'hungry ghost', i.e., what in Pali is called a *peta* and in Sanskrit a *preta*. There are two books in the *Khuddaka Nikāya*, a section of the Pali Canon, the *Petavatthu* and the *Vimāna-vatthu*, which concern particular spirits of the dead; to the Westerner these rather crude works may well seem superfluous. Surely the sufferings of the *peta* could be accommodated in hell? And why are the virtuous subjects of the *Vimāna-vatthu*, in their stereotyped celestial carriages, singled out from others who are reborn in a heaven?

The answer lies here among mortuary rites. While the Buddha taught that rituals were pointless, and laid out a life for the ordained in

---

9 This word literally means 'gone forth'; compare the use of 'passed on' in English. We have discussed elsewhere (Richard F. Gombrich, *Precept and Practice* [Oxford: Clarendon Press, 1971], p. 163) how this word became confused with Sanskrit *pitṛ* ('father' or 'ancestor') and its derivatives, with interesting consequences, which however need not be explained in the present context.

10 Gillian Evison, 'Indian death rituals: The enactment of ambivalence', D.Phil. thesis, Oxford University, 1989, p. 79. We are much indebted to this fine thesis, which alas remains unpublished.

which the part played by ritual was minimal, he did not try to interfere with any lay customs that did not involve violence, such as animal sacrifice. Though there is very little mention in the canon of lay ritual, one can probably deduce from the emperor Asoka's edicts[11] that rituals involving extravagant expenditure (as mortuary rites sometimes did) also met with his disapproval. In one text[12] a Brahmin says to the Buddha that Brahmins practise funerary rituals in which they pray that the gifts that they give to the officiating Brahmins (which must include food) may by this means be enjoyed by the dead, and he asks whether this really works. The Buddha's initial reply is that it does not work if the dead relative is reborn in hell, as an animal, as a human or as a god, but it does work if he is reborn as a *preta*, in which case he lives on what his kinsmen supply. This is Brahmin orthodoxy. When asked further, the Buddha replies that the relatives who *are pretas* will enjoy the actual offering instead, and it can never be the case that one has no relatives who have been reborn as *pretas* – but in any case no act of giving can fail to have a result. This implies that the custom should be continued. In this text there is no mention of the transfer of merit, so the Buddha is simply telling the Brahmin what he expects and hopes to hear: that the objects (food, etc.) donated do pass to the dead and are enjoyed in much the same way as they would be by living human beings.

This suggests that what became the standard Buddhist response to this situation, the transfer of merit, was probably devised and followed towards the end of the Buddha's life. The transfer of merit is an ingenious doctrine which came to permeate the whole of Buddhist practice in every Buddhist tradition. Since the moral quality of an act resides solely in the intention behind it, one might deduce that if I sincerely wish to give someone a dollar, the good karma I have thereby earned is not affected by whether in the end I give it or not. That would not, however, be a correct interpretation, because, just as in English law, whether an intention is carried out cannot be left out of account, and it is assumed that the intention was greater if it was acted on – just as murder is a worse crime than manslaughter.

The Buddha's emphasis on intention has however also had a further result which initially may surprise us, though it is not illogical. A good intention may evoke a similar good intention in an onlooker, and the

---

11   Notably Rock Edict IX.
12   *Aṅguttara Nikāya* V, pp. 269–73 = sutta CLXXVII.

latter thereby earns as much merit as the first intender.[13] Thus, if I intend to give a poor man a dollar, someone who learns of my intention may come to feel equally generous and thus develop an intention just like mine – regardless of whether the intention is finally carried out.

The result recalls the English expression 'having your cake and eating it'. If I want to feed my parents, whether they be alive or dead, that good intention contributes to my store of merit. If someone then learns of my feelings and is inspired to imitate them, they acquire merit too – though this takes away none of my merit. The practical consequence is that when I do something good, or even just intend to do it, I should inform others about my feelings, because that will inspire them to earn merit for themselves. To hide one's light under a bushel is thus worse than pointless.

The English term 'transfer of merit' is seriously misleading, because nothing gets transferred; but it is just like lighting one candle from another. One must remember that in Brahminism/Hinduism one can expunge bad karma from one's record by performing a penance, but this is not so in Buddhism: as mentioned above, the only way to avoid paying for bad karma is to acquire enough good karma to outweigh it, and mortuary rites give the dead an opportunity for creating good karma by witnessing generous acts and emulating the intentions behind them.

When merit transference is mentioned, it is all too easy to be misled by the metaphor into talking as if merit were like money, something one can accumulate in a bank account – and many Buddhists do appear to think of it like that. The historian Richard Seaford has argued that the widespread use of money in ancient India came about in the same period as the Buddhist teaching of karma. He writes that the 'metaphysics of money' involves 'the belief that we are primarily individual agents and only secondarily (if at all) members of a larger [social] entity …'. 'The power of money can increase independence even from deity …'.[14] It is possible that there is an element of coincidence here, because both the teaching of 'the transfer of merit' and the increase in the use of money can be explained independently; nevertheless, the fact that both seem

---

13 In Pali doing an act of merit which is aimed to inspire another is called *patti*; gratefully accepting that opportunity is called *pattānumodanā*.
14 Richard Seaford, *Money and the Early Greek Mind* (Cambridge: Cambridge University Press, 2004), p. 293, cited in Gombrich, *What the Buddha Thought*, pp. 24–25.

to have occurred in the Buddha's environment late in his lifetime, near the end of the fifth century BC, cannot but impress the historian.

It is customary for Buddhists to feed monks, if possible in one's own home, at certain fixed intervals of time after the death of a relative. In Sinhala these are all called *mataka dānēs*, meaning that they are given for the dead.[15] Though the food is offered to the monks with the thought that their consuming it is tantamount to its being consumed by the *preta*(s), giving to the Saṅgha and transferring the merit of that act came to be seen as more reliable than the simple act of providing food and drink. The stated purpose of the *Petavatthu* was 'to establish the superior merit of making gifts to the Buddhist Holy Order and their efficacy as a means of releasing the *pretas* from their state of woe'.[16] The 'transfer' is making a statement (aloud or sotto voce) in which the person who is 'making' merit, for example by giving food to the Saṅgha, calls the attention of a third party, such as the ghost (*preta*) of a recently dead family member, to what is going on, so that the *preta* uses this opportunity to empathise with the donor and enter into the same state of mind, thinking 'How I would like myself to be offering food to the Saṅgha!'

While a *preta* has little or no opportunity to perform meritorious actions independently, its[17] acquisition of merit through a thought process is not confined to a ritual occasion. In the *Majjhima Nikāya*, in a list of recommendations of how a monk should behave, the Buddha says: 'If a monk should wish that it bring great advantage to his dead kinsmen to recollect him with faith in their hearts, he should fulfil the precepts, ... not neglect meditation ...'[18] and the commentator says: 'If the dead relative acquires faith in the virtue of his monastic kinsman and just recollects him, that is capable of keeping the deceased from an evil rebirth for many thousands of *kalpas* and causing him finally to reach the deathless state'.[19] This surely added a new dimension to the 'transfer of merit'.

This is not the end of the historian's story about the transfer of merit; on the contrary, it is the beginning. The next chapter of the

---

15 Gombrich, *Precept and Practice*, p. 229.
16 B.C. Law, *The Buddhist Conception of Spirits* (London: Luzac, 1936), p. 15, cited in Welch, *The Practice of Chinese Buddhism*, p. 181.
17 Remember, a *preta* can be feminine, as befits a belief concerned with karma rather than with ancestors.
18 *Ākaṅkheyya Sutta*, MN I, p. 33, lines 20-23.
19 *Papañcasūdanī* I, pp. 159-60.

story concerns the gods. In Theravāda Buddhism, the population of the heavens (except for the very highest ones) consists of gods, but these gods are unlike what adherents of other religions think of as gods. Just as a virtuous person may receive a reward for their virtue by being reborn as a fortunate (e.g. rich) person in this world, an even more virtuous person may go one better by being reborn in heaven. Conditions in heaven are excellent but not perfect; for instance, the life span of a god is long but finite, and at death they rejoin the cycle in which all other living beings are entrapped – until they finally evade rebirth by attaining nirvana.

While karma, both good and bad, is as it were the motor that drives the cosmic mechanism of transmigration, we learnt from our Theravādin informants in Sri Lanka that the gods who populate the heavens are not thought of as making merit – in which they resemble those who are suffering in hell. Those who follow Obeyesekere's analysis of the development of karma theory will find this easy to understand: originally, before Buddhism, heavens and hells were thought of as places or conditions in which one received the pay-off for what one had done on earth, not as places where one generated fresh karma; after receiving the pay-off one was reborn on earth and started again, as it were, with a blank account. Therefore this Theravādin view of the matter is a historical memory – though those who adhere to it are not aware of why they do so.

Thus unaware, they resort to other explanations which they find consistent with Buddhist cosmology. When we did fieldwork in Sri Lanka, our informants told us that life in heaven is too comfortable, causing heaven-dwellers to forget the basic truth that all life is *dukkha* (unsatisfactory).[20] This then becomes used as a justification for the Theravādin custom of transferring one's merit to the gods after performing any act of piety; they cannot earn merit for themselves, so we must do it for them, drawing their attention to what we are doing so that they can gain merit by empathy.

We suspect that there may be yet another reason underlying it – again a historical one: that in this culture, when one asks a spirit to bestow a material benefit, one promises that if the request is granted

---

20 Similarly, it is believed that nirvana can only be attained while living in this human world – though here too there is an inconsistency: this restriction does not apply to those in the heavens higher than the heavens of the gods (*deva-loka*).

one will respond with a *quid pro quo*, as normally occurs in relationships between humans. Initially in Buddhism the gods were inherited from the cultural environment as part of the cosmic furniture and played no part in the soteriology. Buddhists believed that there existed in most (perhaps all) societies many powerful superhuman beings who lived in heavens or on earth (or both) and had the power to grant petitionary prayers/requests; these beings were known by words which are commonly and reasonably translated as 'gods'.

We are not aware that the matter is discussed in any ancient text, so it is possible that all three explanations are correct. However, the third one is to our mind the least likely. Even in cases where they were perhaps not able to theorize about it, the Buddhists who believed in and might pray to those gods were vividly aware of the distinction between petitionary and spiritual prayer[21] and knew that the two categories demanded completely different attitudes and behaviour. In brief, a spiritual good, which typically concerns one's own death and future lives, can be attained only by one's own efforts. A superior being, such as the Buddha, may help one to attain it, but that help takes the form of wise advice (often from a holy man) which explains what one can do to help oneself.

Be that as it may, this technique which permits the gods to acquire merit is virtually the same as is applied to the recently dead. The intended results, however, are different: the gods in return are supposed to give people protection and grant their wishes for this life. So, the positive functions which Brahmin/Hindu ideology ascribes to ancestors (though gods may share these functions as well), are firmly assigned by the Buddhists to gods. In the Buddhist interaction with *pretas*, however, the benefits flow the other way.

In Sanskrit the equivalent of 'petitionary' (goods or requests) is *laukika*, literally 'worldly', and the equivalent of 'spiritual' is *lokottara*, literally 'supramundane'. These words and their translations into local languages are not confined to talk about prayer but used in many contexts.

In the nineteenth and twentieth centuries the Westerners, often agents of the Christian colonial powers, who first observed Buddhist societies were in many cases seriously confused. Finding that local Buddhist populations believed in gods and interacted with them, they criticized them for being bad Buddhists who had lost sight of the

---

21 See our 'Preamble', above, n. 17.

Buddha's teachings. Only until quite recently, when scholars began to point out that in the earliest scriptures, notably the Pali Canon, gods played a similar role to that which they play today, did they come to realize their misunderstanding; but this clarification has still not reached all the authors of textbooks and works of reference.

The practice of transferring merit led to a watershed in the history of Buddhism. Originally, one could only receive merit by wanting to do so and empathizing with an act of merit which one knew about. But in the Mahāyāna the standard way of transferring one's own act of merit was by expressing the wish that it accrue to the credit of all living beings – whether they were aware of it or not. The crucial link between karma and intention was thus broken. Merit could still be created by a meritorious intention, but over and above this it also floated around the universe in a way reminiscent of how we imagine luck.

The proliferation of the transfer of merit created the salient features which have characterized Mahāyāna Buddhism ever since. If one could so easily acquire merit through some act of empathy, without even being aware of it, this weakened the rigour of the Buddha's teaching that we are solely and wholly responsible for our own karma. In the Mahāyāna, supernatural figures, whether called Buddhas, bodhisattvas or gods, could both acquire and distribute merit as they pleased, and could do this in any situation anywhere in the universe. A comparativist may be forgiven for claiming that despite obscuring the cosmology by introducing many categories of living beings and sophisticated ontologies, Mahāyāna Buddhism became a polytheism.[22]

In discussing Buddhism in China, Francisca Cho has written:

> The way in which Buddhist ritual provided a way to enhance the indigenous practice of ancestor worship is particularly interesting. The institution of Buddhist monasticism, with its order of celibate monks, seriously clashed with the Chinese concern with preserving and perpetuating the family line. But in the Buddhist ritual system, supporting the monastic order with economic necessities created merit (good karmic fruit) for the donor that could be transferred to his ancestors, ensuring auspicious circumstances in their new lives. Hence an inherently offensive social institution was brilliantly transformed by the Buddhist cosmology of rebirth into a most potent

---

22 Whether one calls non-Mahāyāna Buddhism 'theistic' is really a matter of choice: certainly it believes in the existence of 'gods', but no less certainly those gods are very unlike the beings that non-Buddhist theists normally believe in.

site for the practice of filial piety. What is particularly noteworthy here is both the fact and the irrelevance of the clashing conceptual structures brought about by this blending of Buddhist and Confucian practice. Buddhist merit was dedicated to ancestors in the belief that it would help them attain auspicious new births. But in Confucian practice, propitiation of ancestors was premised on the belief that ancestral spirits hovered and remained close to the living, with the power to bring them fortune or harm. Do ancestors remain with the living, or do they reincarnate? For the Chinese practitioners, resolving the question was of less importance than the added ritual technology for practicing filial piety, which assured the well-being of the living.[23]

What she describes in China could have been written almost word for word about Buddhism in India and the Theravāda tradition. For 'Chinese' read 'Indian', for 'Confucian' read 'Brahminical'; the variations are trivial. Her eloquence should not blind us to the fact that the 'brilliant transformation' she refers to took place almost a millennium earlier than she thinks, and it is highly probable that its main features can be ascribed to the Buddha himself.

Appendix

Collective karma in China

(a) Xinran, *China Witness* (London: Chatto & Windus, 2008), pp. 1–2.

The concept of guilt by association, Professor Gao Mingxuan, an authority on the Chinese penal code, has remarked, was always very important in ancient Chinese law. As early as the second millennium BC, a criminal's family was punished as harshly as the criminal himself. Over the next thousand years, this principle steadily tightened its grip on the judicial system. In his canonical history of China, written around 100 BC, Sima Qian recorded that 'after Shang Yang ordered changes in the law [c.350BC], the people were grouped in units of five and ten households, carrying out military surveillance, and mutually responsible for each other's conduct before the law'. If a member of one family committed a crime, the other families in that unit were

---

23 Francisca Cho, 'Buddhism and science: Translating and re-translating culture', in David L. McMahan (ed.), *Buddhism in the Modern World* (Abingdon and New York: Routledge, 2012), p. 277, cited in Gombrich and Yao, 'A radical Buddhism for modern Confucians', p. 254.

judged to be guilty by association. By the Qin dynasty (221–206 BC), the principle was applied not only within communities, but also within the army and government. In the case of minor offences, the criminal's family would be exterminated to between three and five degrees of association; with serious offences, to nine to ten. Although the virtues of this penal principle were debated at various points in the imperial past, it remained a mainstay of the Chinese judicial code until the Ming and Qing dynasties (1368–1911).

(b) Email from Ven. Śrāvastī Dhammika to Richard Gombrich, 4 January 2015.

In recent decades something referred to as collective kamma or group kamma has been posited and discussed. According to this theory, groups of people or even a whole nation can supposedly suffer the results (as usual, positive collective kamma never seems to be discussed, it's always negative kamma). The revered Tibetan master Lati Rimpoche recently claimed that the suffering of the Jewish people during the Holocaust was the result of great wickedness they had all committed in previous lives. Others have claimed that the murderous rule of the Khmer Rouge was likewise kammic retribution for past evil done by the Cambodian people.

Nothing explicitly mentioning the idea of collective kamma is found in the Buddha's teachings and there is no Pali or Sanskrit term for collective kamma in the traditional lexicons. The idea also seems to be absent from later Buddhist texts. However, in his *Abhidharmakośabhāṣya* Vasubandhu has a comment that could be interpreted as suggesting collective kamma. He says: 'When many persons are united with the intention to kill, either in war, or in the hunt, or in banditry, who is guilty of murder, if only one of them kills? As soldiers, etc., concur in the realization of the same effect, all are as guilty as is the one who kills. Having a common goal, all are guilty just as he who among them kills, for all mutually incite one another, not through speech, but by the very fact that they are united together in order to kill. But is the person who has been constrained through force to join the army also guilty? Evidently so, unless he has formed the resolution: "Even in order to save my life, I shall not kill a living being"'.[24] If indeed Vasubandhu was positing

---

24 Vasubandhu, *Abhidharmakośabhāṣya*, Vol. 1, translated into French by Louis de La Vallée Poussin, English translation by Leo M. Pruden (Berkeley, CA: Asian Humanities Press, 1991), p. 649.

collective kamma the example he gave for it is not very convincing. Let us consider it carefully. All the persons mentioned in this example would have come together with a common negative purpose and thus would have all committed some negative kamma, as Vasubandhu correctly says. However, the nature and intensity of their individual intentions may well have varied. Some might have been enthusiastic about what was planned, others less so, one or two may have had serious reservations. Further, the kammic background of each person would have been different. One could have been a hardened criminal who had committed many crimes before, another might have been a novice in crime, while a third might have been basically good but weak and easily led by his friends. With such a variety of motives and backgrounds, how each member of the gang would have felt and acted subsequent to their crime is likely to have been just as diverse, ranging all the way from cruel satisfaction, to cold indifference, to regret. Taking all these quite plausible and even quite likely differences into consideration, it is only realistic to imagine that the *vipāka* of each person in the group would be of very different strength and that it would manifest at different times and in very different ways. Thus a second look at this passage will show that it is not a convincing argument for collective kamma, if indeed that is what it is meant to be.

One incident from the Buddhist tradition that could be suggesting something like collective kamma is a story about the Sakyans, the Buddha's kinsmen. Viḍūḍabha, the king of Kosala, massacred 'all the Sakyans' including even 'the suckling babes', and they suffered this fate supposedly because 'the Sakyans' had some time previously poisoned a river in a dispute over its water (Ja.IV,152). In reality, only a few Sakyans would have committed this evil deed, and although the Sakyan chiefs probably authorized it and a number of others may have approved of it, the majority, particularly the babies and children, would have had nothing to do with it. Thus the idea of collective kamma is implicit in this story. How are we to explain this? The story is not in the *Tipiṭaka* but comes from the *Jātaka* commentary, a text of uncertain but late date. Some scholars consider it to have been composed in Sri Lanka rather than India. But whoever the author was it seems likely that he was just storytelling, rather than positing the idea of collective kamma as a specific doctrine. The fact that no later commentators took the story as a cue to develop the idea of collective kamma strengthens this assumption. Also, another version of the story, from the *Mahāvaṃsa Ṭīkā*, says that there were survivors of the massacre, thus undermining that claim that 'all Sakyans' suffered the negative *vipāka* of the kamma created by others.

The version of collective kamma which maintains that the consequences of deeds done by some within a group can be experienced by others within the same group, contradicts one of the most fundamental Buddhist concepts; that each individual is responsible for themselves.

The earliest unambiguous mention of collective kamma that I have been able to find is in the writings of the nineteenth-century occultist Helena Blavatsky. In her *The Key to Theosophy*, 1889, Blavatsky makes reference to what she called 'National Karma'. The idea seems to have subsequently been taken up by various believers in the occult, then absorbed into New Age thinking, from where it has spread to Buddhism. It is surprising how many Buddhist teachers, learned and otherwise, speak of collective kamma as if it were a part of authentic Dhamma, despite its recent origin and it having no precedent in traditional Buddhism.

Figure 3: Monastic lectures to pilgrims on a guided tour of the HQ, Gaoxiong, 25 December 2020

Chapter 4

HSING YUN'S ETHOS AND ACTIVITIES

The ethos of FGS compared to that of Tzu Chi

To attempt to characterize the ethos of a human group or institution is usually hazardous. If one posits a contrast with a norm, what is that norm? One must also be cautious about making judgments which overgeneralize, not leaving enough room for exceptional individuals or occasions.

When we wish to give our readers a feel for the ethos of such a large and varied organization as FGS, the problem seems acute. However, the case presents two features which appear helpful. The first is that the single figure of its founder, Master Hsing Yun, looms so large, his influence on the movement is so ubiquitous and his pronouncements are so many and so explicit, that he permeates the movement's ethos, rendering its description a relatively straightforward enterprise.

The second feature is that there exists a movement which it would be helpful to contrast with FGS. Tzu Chi is a Taiwanese Buddhist movement of much the same age as FGS. Like FGS, it has been enormously successful within Taiwan and has also spread worldwide, with branches in many other countries. It has become a commonplace among those who write about Buddhism in Taiwan since the end of World War II that there are three movements of 'Humanistic Buddhism': FGS, Tzu Chi, and Dharma Drum, founded by the Ven. Sheng Yen (1931–2009). The founders of all three movements were born at about the same time and have lived to be very old; Sheng Yen is however the only one who is now dead.

It happens that both authors of this book have studied and published about Tzu Chi. This enables us to appreciate an admirable article by Prof. Richard Madsen called 'Practice not dogma: Tzu-chi and the

Buddhist tradition'.[1] Though he does not use the word, Madsen gives a perceptive account of the Tzu Chi ethos. Madsen's first point is that Tzu Chi has a clearcut single focus: compassion. That focus is a matter of action, not theory. In both respects, this is in contrast to FGS. Master Cheng Yen, founder and leader of Tzu Chi, is known for saying, 'Just do it'. In the library of Tzu-chi's headquarters is a collection of binders documenting all the works of compassion that Tzu-chi members have carried out. Madsen was told, 'These are our sutras'. Nothing but actual acts of compassion has much relevance.

FGS is quite different. As is true of many Buddhist traditions, if asked, 'What is Buddhism essentially about?' a knowledgeable spokesman for FGS would have to say that it is about a lot of things, such as enlightenment, meditation, morality, respect, understanding, generosity ... and so on. Education, particularly knowledge of Buddhist texts, is regarded as extremely important, particularly for members of the Saṅgha, who are indeed ranked largely by their educational qualifications. Hsing Yun founded a seminary before any other major Buddhist buildings or institutions. He strongly encourages knowledge, and creation of Buddhist art, music and literature.

'The practice of Buddhist compassion was traditionally directed not to abstract categories of people but to individual persons. It did not seek to change social structures but to help one individual at a time. ... When handing out food and clothing to victims of disasters, Tzu-chi volunteers do so individually, face to face, if possible while looking the recipient directly in the eyes and bowing in a gesture of respect'.[2] Tzu Chi's 'forms of giving ... are not in the short run as efficient or cost-effective as the best practices of many NGOs. But bodhisattva compassion is not about costs, it is about personal engagement with others that can lead both giver and recipient to expand their minds and hearts to develop ever fuller degrees of compassion'.[3]

Tzu Chi does not cultivate irrationality, but in the activities which constitute its focus, it is the heart that leads, not the brain. Compassion is above all an emotion, and is to be felt strongly enough to drive action.

---

1 Richard Madsen, 'Practice not dogma: Tzu-chi and the Buddhist tradition', *Journal of the Oxford Centre for Buddhist Studies* 16 (May 2019): 87–97. No less admirable is Madsen's earlier article, 'Tzu Chi: The modernization of Buddhist compassion', in Madsen, *Democracy's Dharma* (Berkeley: University of California Press, 2007), chapter 2, pp. 16–50.
2 Madsen, 'Practice not dogma', pp. 89–90.
3 Ibid., p. 90.

Tzu Chi is by no means puritanical, but it is equally distant from the jollity which Hsing Yun encourages among his followers and often himself takes part in.

It can hardly be a coincidence that Tzu Chi was founded and is led by a woman, whereas FGS was founded and is led by a man. The fact that the Saṅgha of FGS consists overwhelmingly of women, not men, can be misleading. The style and substance of the lives of FGS Saṅgha members are masculine in tone. Moreover, while members of both movements practise their Buddhism by reaching out into the world, the public engagement of an FGS member is a role performance, generally not directed at particular individuals.

On the other hand, one could argue that in terms of actual personnel both movements have in various ways reflected that tendency to recruit into their Saṅghas far more women than men which we found when we investigated the importance of their Japanese roots as long ago as the early twentieth century. Not only are more women recruited, but they also have been easier to retain than men; and while the top places in the hierarchy often go to men, at the levels below the top women preponderate.[4]

Madsen draws contrasting sketches of the spirit in which Tzu Chi and FGS operate in action.

> Tzu Chi has ... evolved into a complicated (and wealthy) corporate organization even as it retains the characteristics of a religious community ... [Its] mission makes no sense outside of the Humanistic Buddhist vision and the Confucian ethic propagated by Cheng Yen. Not only its members, but also its professional staff, speak of it as a family bound together by ties of love and commitment, and dedicated to following the bodhisattva path of spreading compassion throughout the world. All of its members see Cheng Yen as a Confucian parent who needs to be consulted on all important issues and whose will is final. When going on international relief missions, for example, they send daily faxes to [the HQ] at Hualien reporting their activities to the Master. ... Most of the volunteer work takes place in an egalitarian spirit with minimal division of labor. Members address one another as Teacher Brother and Teacher Sister ... and wear uniforms that suppress any signs of worldly status.[5]

---

4 For the Japanese roots see Yao, 'Japanese influence on Buddhism in Taiwan', pp. 141–56; for the resort to Japan to train the lower leadership of FGS see Yao and Gombrich, 'Telescope and microscope', pp. 128–55, particularly pp. 135–39.

5 Madsen, *Democracy's Dharma*, p. 39.

As Madsen shows at length, the ethos of FGS is far less clearly differentiated from the style and mores of the workaday world.

> Hsing Yun has many friends among the business class, the military, and the popular culture circles. In line with the teaching of Chan masters, he tells all such people to play their roles as best they can: to be honest, valiant, and creative. He does not necessarily confront the difficulties of doing this in a globalized world. For example, success in a global economy requires participating in competition that is much more intense than what was found in the premodern economies in which traditional Buddhist teaching was formulated. ... Success in global politics ... requires amassing military assets. Success in a commercialized global culture requires producing slick entertainment. Hsing Yun's popularity is based on not placing impossible ... demands on people enmeshed in modern worldly systems of wealth and power. He only asks that people act with good intentions, and try to lessen the greed, violence, and beguilement that are part and parcel of their work. Although [his] views about moral ideals are both clear and conservative, he does not make firm pronouncements about how followers should balance ideals with the demands of reality. ... [What he] promotes is a fuzzy ambiguous social consensus that allows for a great plurality of interpretation among people in different circumstances.[6]

As indicated above, it is the character of FGS's Master which overwhelmingly sets the tone. To understand his personality, we need to look into his biography.

Hsing Yun's early life

Hsing Yun was born in Jiang-du, in Jiang-Su province, in 1927, the second son of Li, who ran a shop selling candles and incense. His mother recalled that during her pregnancy she dreamed that a little golden man stood by her bed, silently looking for something, and a grey-haired man told her that he was looking for rice seed, *dao-suei* in Chinese. These words can also mean 'teachings'.[7] The mother replied, 'There is no rice under my bed, only straw'. But then the little man gave her rice seed, and the grey-haired man said, 'From this you will receive fruit (*otao*)'.

---

6 Ibid., pp. 80-81.
7 Zhi Yin Fu, *Chuan Din: Biography of Hsing Yun* (Taipei: Tian-Xia, 2nd ed., 1996), p. 10. Fu's book is based on personal interviews with the Master and others who knew him very well.

When Hsing Yun was born, one half of his face was red, the other white; and on the middle of his upper lip there was a line from his nose to his mouth. His mother kept him close to her in order not to shock people, who might fear he was a monster; but the line disappeared soon afterwards.

Hsing Yun was about ten when the Japanese invaded. It was hard to buy the necessaries of life. The family lived by a river, and only a few dared to go out, but the boy would swim across and return with what was needed. This gained him a great local reputation.

Hsing Yun received no formal education until he was eight years old. Then he was given some education locally for a while, and learnt to read, but the Japanese occupation and the poverty and consequent criminality of the area made life very unstable.

In his biography Hsing Yun remembers living with his mother's mother. She was illiterate, but hardworking, dignified and compassionate. She had become a vegetarian when aged 18, and would chant sutras including the *Diamond Sūtra* and the *Amitābha Sūtra*. Sometimes she meditated during the night. Hsing Yun shared her meals and joined her in meditation. She took Hsing Yun and his sister to visit Buddhist temples and then gave them sweets, which made him enjoy such trips. She was sometimes visited by Buddhist masters, and Hsing Yun began to feel the attraction of being a Buddhist monk.[8]

In 1937 his father went away in search of work and had been gone for two years. His mother took him to Nanjing, looking for her husband. The great Japanese massacre took place that December. His father was never found and may have died in the massacre. On the way to Nanjing they were approached by a monk, who asked Hsing Yun whether he would like to become a monk, and he firmly said he would. Soon after this the abbot of Qixia monastery, Ven Zhi Kai, informed him by messenger that he was willing to be his master. He was tonsured in Qixia, a public temple, but Zhi Kai was from Da Jui, so Hsing Yun followed his master, as was the custom, and his home temple too became Da Jui, and he was in the 48th generation of Lin Ji's lineage.

More than 400 monks lived in Qixia temple. Because of the Japanese invasion, their standard of living was very austere, to say the least. Hsing Yun for over a year could not even obtain the money to buy a postage stamp to send his mother a letter. He had no shoes or socks, no new clothes, and no water for washing. Food was very limited and often

---

8   Fu, *Chuan Din*, pp. 12–13.

rotten, and there was rice only once a fortnight; even then it had stones and worms in it. Medical care was a rare luxury. When he had malaria, despite being extremely ill, he was not allowed a day off but had to attend the services. (This was because he was in a public monastery.) His master eventually heard of his sickness. Being the dean of a Buddhist college, he was able to order someone to send his pupil half a bowl of salted pickle – a favour that Hsing Yun found very moving. He vowed that beside propagating Buddhism, he would improve the Saṅgha's living conditions and distribute food to hungry people. This is why he has always ensured that his monasteries are built with large kitchens.

His master treated him with iron discipline, even though he was his only disciple, and just 12 years old at that time. When he listened to his master's preaching he had to kneel on stone floors for three or four hours; sometimes stones penetrated his muscles. At 15 he was fully ordained, and experienced ruthless treatment which was meted out as a policy. During the 53-day period in which he was taught the monastic precepts, he was given trick questions and physically punished, including blows to the head, for whatever answer he gave. He reacted to this treatment by concluding that it was important in life to be both resilient and flexible, and not to depend on externals.

For ten years his master never allowed Hsing Yun to go home and never treated him with any warmth, or conferred on him any praise, only criticism. In that time he gave him only two pieces of cloth, a small supplement to his normal robes. Looking back on this experience forty years later, Hsing Yun said that he now realized that his master treated him like that because he had such high expectations of him.

In 1945, when he was 18, World War II ended and the Japanese left. After six years in Qixia, Hsing Yun was admitted to Jiaoshan Buddhist seminary in Zhenjiang. He began to study the *Abhidharmakośabhāṣya*,[9] Yogācāra, and original Buddhism. His teacher remembered him as very quiet and hardworking. Though his seminary had no interest at all in teaching anything Western, and did not even take a newspaper, Hsing Yun was full of curiosity, and managed to visit school libraries where he could find copies of Chinese classics and sources of information about the West and the modern world, including Chinese translations of European books. He became passionate about the importance of books and reading, and even spent money he needed for food on

---

9 A classic compendium of doctrinal tenets composed in Sanskrit by Vasubandhu some time round 400 AD.

buying books; later, when he acquired pupils himself, he was always giving them books. He also realized that the defeat of the Japanese was essential if Buddhism was to survive in China.

In 1947 he became manager of his home temple in Da Jui, and then principal of Baita elementary school. He and a friend founded a Buddhist magazine called *Angry Wave* (*Nu Tao*), and he also edited the local newspaper. In this period local control alternated between communists and nationalists (GMD), and Hsing Yun found himself briefly imprisoned by each side in turn.

At that time many young people looked down on both Confucianism and Buddhism as old-fashioned and superstitious. Many converted to Christianity, and warlords destroyed Buddhist temples and defrocked and even murdered monks, even before the communists came to power. In this crisis the only master he found as a guide was Tai Xu, who had long been advocating that Buddhism reform itself in many ways, but above all by becoming less pessimistic and not making the idea that life is suffering the central focus of its doctrine. Tai Xu also identified the fortunes of Buddhism with those of the Chinese nation. Hsing Yun became a devoted follower of Tai Xu and adopted his motto never to think of what Buddhism can do for you, only of what you can do for Buddhism; he also adopted his view that the evil destiny of China and hence of Buddhism was grounded in poverty and ignorance.

In 1949 the KMT government of Jiang Jie Shi (= Chiang Kai Shek) was defeated and fled to Taiwan. Hsing Yun and other Buddhist monks at first organized themselves into a medical team to attend the defeated soldiers, but then a group of 70 of them went to Taiwan in the hope of preserving Buddhism. Though they came to Taiwan as refugees, virtually penniless, they were widely regarded with suspicion and most temples refused to admit them. Hsing Yun was even imprisoned (for the third time in his life) on suspicion of being a communist spy, but an influential Buddhist lady,[10] wife of a general, got him released after only 23 days. Finally Ven. Miao Guo, the abbot of a temple in Zhong Li called Yuan Guang, sheltered Hsing Yun, and he stayed there for two years performing onerous menial tasks. Though he had to work dreadfully hard, he managed while there to begin writing his first book, *Silent Song* (*Wu Shen Xi der Gechang*), and to edit the magazine *Life* (*Ren Sheng*).

---

10 This is Sun Zhang Qing Yang, who became a lifelong supporter of FGS. For details see Yao and Gombrich, 'Telescope and microscope', p. 142.

Only when he went to Yilan in 1952 did he acquire the independence to participate in the proselytizing activities which finally led to his founding of FGS. However, it was some years before he was entirely trusted by the government, and he used to begin his sermons by declaring himself a supporter of Jian Jie Shi. This led to his converting to Buddhism the secret police who were keeping track of him.

Hsing Yun's ethos and concerns

It is at this point, when he was in his late twenties, that Hsing Yun's proselytizing activities really began and set the tone for FGS, which he went on to found in 1967. From then on, writes his biographer, he would compose about ten thousand words a day.[11] We shall now give a rather summary account of those activities over approximately the next 30 years, and follow that by a similar account of FGS rituals. Both accounts depend primarily on the FGS yearbook for 1987, a few sections of which we have translated into English with some abbreviations and occasional notes intended either for clarification or simply to make the account more up to date.

The best account of the message he has been transmitting would obviously be in his own words. However, the bibliography of his books, articles and speeches published in 2017 on the home page of the Buddha Memorial Centre lists 365 volumes containing (they say) 50,000 entries and 30 million words. Though a small proportion of these compositions have been translated (and are not included in the above figures), most of them are accessible only to readers of Chinese, and our account is intended for a much wider public.

We think that even without our constantly drawing attention to them, a superficial listing of Hsing Yun's activities will show attentive readers that certain themes are salient. They can be roughly divided between those which he inherited (explicitly) from Tai Xu, and those which he mainly contributed himself. His debt to Tai Xu we summarize early in part 2 of our article 'Christianity as model and analogue in the formation of "Humanistic" Buddhism'.

The very term 'Humanistic Buddhism' was taken over (with a small change) from Tai Xu by Hsing Yun. A variant name for it was 'Buddhism for Human Life'. First and foremost, the name indicates that Buddhism,

---

11 Fu, *Chuan Din*, p. 73.

as these great reformers found it, was far too preoccupied with death and its aftermath, and not nearly enough with the daily lives of ordinary people. This in turn implies three crucial attitudes: that Buddhists should try to concentrate much less on grief and suffering and adopt a more positive attitude to life; that they should be active in the here and now, and concern themselves with philosophy only when it was pragmatic; and that monks and nuns should care not just for their own spiritual progress but also for social and even political issues, and regard themselves as responsible for the advancement of Buddhism, not just leaving such matters to the laity. Pursuing this line of thought further, Humanistic Buddhism agrees with Tai Xu that the two most important sources of evil and suffering are poverty and ignorance, and from this it follows that education is of extreme importance, and that one should appreciate the benefits that modernity has to offer, both through advanced technology and through the wider range of knowledge and understanding now available to us, for instance through television and the internet. This broadening of our horizons brings benefits and opportunities, and has been welcomed by Tai Xu and Hsing Yun, but at the same time both of them are Chinese patriots, particularly concerned with the condition of Chinese Buddhism and Chinese culture.

Humanistic Buddhism is Mahāyāna, attaching great importance to compassion and spiritual egalitarianism. It distinguishes itself from the older form of Buddhism, Theravāda. It tends to believe that the ethos of Theravāda is selfish and inward-looking. While this view is mainly based on a serious misunderstanding,[12] it does affect the ideological stance. However, we must immediately qualify this observation by adding that in practice there is little polemics to be seen and vaunting the superiority of the Mahāyāna is generally confined to the classroom.

The stress on the individual as against the collective can take very different forms. At the beginning of this chapter we drew attention to how Tzu Chi, which is not merely Mahāyāna but also widely labelled as 'Humanistic Buddhism', stresses the crucial importance of individual involvement, which must be manifested in action. Consonant with this, when Master Cheng Yen, Tzu Chi's founder, set out on her first great fundraising enterprise, to finance the building of a hospital in the remote area where she lived, a Japanese offered to pay for the whole thing but she turned his offer down, because she attached such importance to giving as many people as possible a chance to act with

---

12 See Gombrich, *What the Buddha Thought*, pp. 77–78.

compassion. Hsing Yun showed exactly the same attitude when he said that he preferred small donations to large ones: the implication that there should be many small ones was obvious. When writing on karma in Chapter 3 we have argued that stress on the individual agent is essential to early Buddhism (and thus to the Theravāda) – but that does not mean that it cannot play a part in Mahāyāna ideology.

Hsing Yun's emphasis on living a full life and enjoying it

A useful entry to this set of themes is HY's attitude to money. In Chapter 2 we quoted a magazine article he wrote about it in 1961.[13] Elsewhere he has written:

> [T]he wise cherish wealth and know the correct way to acquire it. For when wealth comes in a proper way, the more the better. No Buddhist should have any cause for resistance against wealth ... Neither one who devalues wealth [n]or a miser is called wise. *Possessing* wealth is a pleasure, but to be able to utilise wealth for the benefit of others is truly *enjoying* wealth.[14]

Buddhism needs to be popularized

Hsing Yun has had a much longer life than Tai Xu and, since the age of about 30, he has fared under less difficult circumstances, so it is not surprising, and rather unfair to the latter, if the range of his achievements seems far greater. In preaching for people to make good use of their lives, he has on many and various occasions stressed not only enjoyment but also education, cultural awareness – including awareness of the modern world, creativity, charity (in the narrower sense), tolerance, and loyalty to Chinese tradition and culture.

In the 1987 yearbook he wrote:[15]

---

13 *Awakening*, 1 October 1961, reprinted in 'Everybody Rich', in *Writings in Awakening*, 1982, pp. 48–50.
14 Quotation from Fo Chi-ying, *Handing Down the Light*, trans. Amy Lui-ma (Hacienda Lights, CA: Xi Lai University Press, 1996), pp. 228–30, in Madsen, *Democracy's Dharma*, p. 70.
15 Fo Guang Shan, *20th Yearbook, 1987*, edited by the Religious Affairs Committee, headed by Shi Xin Ping (Gaoxiong: Fo Guang Shan, 1987), pp. 329ff. The following sections on publications, radio, TV and 'islandwide propagation' are

4 guidelines for FGS:

1. Buddhism needs to be popularised. People have come to chant or pray, but most of them have been very old. FGS has to show that Buddhism is not just for the old. Organise dharma meeting activities. The average age of members since FGS's foundation (20 years ago) has been reduced by 20 years.[16]
2. Buddhism should be for daily life. People used to see it as pessimistic, a way of avoiding the real world in preparation for death; it comes to mind when one is frustrated or helpless. People in trouble seek the help of a bodhisattva, especially when a relative has died. By contrast, *FGS is for life, not for death.*
3. Buddhists should be artistic. Use the arts to promote Buddhism. Buddhist art is at the core of Chinese culture, which is to be shown and continued by FGS architecture, museums and exhibitions, and by applying aesthetic criteria to all we do.
4. Buddhism must create its own literature, not just philosophy. He uses elegant words in his speeches and writings, to show he has a deep knowledge of Buddhist literature. [At the same time, they should be easy to understand.] FGS publications will be well written and contribute to raising society's cultural level.

He aimed to teach the music and songs of the dharma. Drama, publications, radio, TV, seminars for the laity, summer camps – all would be modernized without losing the traditional spirit. He would purify society by bringing in the dharma everywhere: he would go into the countryside, to the army, to factories, to prisons – not only in Taiwan and China but anywhere in the world.

We have argued in Chapter 2 that Hsing Yun's insistence that people, including monastics, should enjoy their lives is at odds with the whole Buddhist tradition. His personal involvement with entertainments such as music, which Buddhist tradition generally proscribes for monastics, and his use of radio and television, are part of this attitude, an attitude which reflects the influence of mainstream Christianity and conveys to its audience a strong flavour of modernity.

Publications

Writing and editing are Hsing Yun's main method for proselytizing, even outweighing preaching, and have always been FGS's main work.

---

all taken from this yearbook. It was almost certainly written by a committee but the Master must have approved it.

16 Later the maximum age for ordination was lowered to 35.

He used his royalties to buy the land for the FGS headquarters. In 1959 he established a Buddhist Cultural Service Office in Taipei, and there published booklets to teach Buddhism simply, and sold aids to Buddhist practice such as reference works and physical items (e.g. robes, bells). He has edited books on Buddhism for children, and published an album of Buddhist songs. His office thus became the FGS publishing house. Its three main tasks are to publish: an FGS *Tripiṭaka* (which adds punctuation to the text); a Buddhist dictionary; and a history of Buddhism.

Since 1968 FGS has had its journal, *Awakening*, published every ten days. No interruption in publication has occurred. There is also the monthly *Universal Gate*, which is thicker, and by 1988 had 100 issues. *Awakening* is largely written by Hsing Yun; *Universal Gate* is a more general Buddhist magazine with articles by many authors and also dealing with Buddhist activities. An FGS newspaper, called 'Merit Time' (*Ren-jian fu-biao*, which means reading it brings you merit) began in April 2000.

Radio and recordings

In 1951 in Yilan, Hsing Yun organized a youth choir at Lei Yin temple, and in 1952 began a chanting society. In 1961 he issued his sixth volume of records of Buddhist chants and holy music, made at the American News Office. (According to Chandler, *Establishing a Pure Land on Earth*, p. 126, cited also in Francesca Tarocco, *The Cultural Practices of Modern Chinese Buddhism: Attuning the Dharma* (London and New York: Routledge, 2007), p. 134: 'Fo-Guang literature boasts that, in 1957, the Master cut the first-ever ten-inch Buddhist record'.)

In 1957 HY began daily radio broadcasts, 7.00–7.30 a.m., from a private radio station in Yilan; the programme, called 'The Sound of Buddhism' (*Fo jiao zhi-she*), included teachings for all and Buddhism for children, chanting, biographies of important monks, and family practice. He took turns with disciples in running the programme, which ran for four years and had much impact. In 1960, on the Buddha's birthday, university students from the whole of Taiwan organized a broadcast competition, for seven days, of Buddhist speeches. In 1961 a chair of Taiwan Radio's Yilan office invited Hsing Yun to run a Buddhist programme from his public station. This was 'The Sound of Awakening', from 6.10 to 6.30 every morning. In 1984 in Xi Lai (Los Angeles) they began broadcasting from 8.00 to 8.30 a.m. on their Chinese language radio station: 'The Buddha's light illuminates the world'. This conveyed to Americans not only Buddhist teaching but also Chinese culture.

TV

In 1962 Taiwan had its first TV station. Hsing Yun organized concerts of Buddhist music, lectures on Buddhism, and other programmes. He himself paid for the time. He had to submit his programme proposals, and the supervisor did not want too much religion or religious propaganda. Also, Hsing Yun was short of suitable human resources. (From 1969 onwards, several of his chief pupils were studying in Japan.[17]) In 1978-79 he made a big push, spending much effort and money. He began a programme called *Gan lou* (*Amṛta - Ambrosia*), to make our world into a heaven. It received an award from the Ministry of Education and the Ministry of the Interior. (This shows that its conservative slant favoured the government.)

In 1980 he created another TV programme called *Xi Xing Men*, 'The Gate of Faith', on another channel. The story is that a little snail gets lost in a field and encounters a travelling monk, whom he accompanies, and this leads to a lot of outdoor photography, introducing the audience to Buddhist temples in China and Taiwan. The snail represents disoriented youth; the monk true knowledge and understanding. There were 100 episodes, each 30 minutes long, and each programme cost Hsing Yun 150,000 NT. The programme answered questions about Buddhism written by the audience. Each week the audience was given a new sentence/phrase from a great monk to memorize, and a Buddhist song was taught. The programme attracted 5 million viewers. For this FGS received an award from the Ministry of Justice.

In November 1983 HY began a series of 30 Buddhist lectures on TV, twice a month, 60 minutes each. These were said to reconcile quarrelling families, who then took the Three Refuges.[18] In 1985 this programme won the Golden Bell award from the Ministry of Culture.

HY divided his 1985 lecture series on the *Platform Sutra* of the 6th Patriarch into 10 themes; there were 65 episodes, each lasting 30 minutes. These were the first ever TV programmes on a Buddhist sutra.

The programme 'Hsing Yun's time talking' (*Xing Yun Chan Hua*) began in 1984, 5 minutes per day in the lunch hour, Monday to Friday. HY

---

17 Details in Yao and Gombrich, 'Telescope and microscope', pp. 135-40.
18 They thus formally became Buddhist laity.

would record up to 80 episodes in one go. He planned a Buddhist TV channel, which began in 1997 and lasted until he was too old to take a major part, called *Ren jia Wei Shi* 'Beautiful Life TV'; he also created a Buddhist film company and a Buddhist soap opera.

Islandwide propagation

In 1955 Hsing Yun began photocopying the Japanese *Tripiṭaka*. He and other Buddhist masters wanted to spread these copies islandwide to devotees. The team leader was his contemporary the Ven. Nan Ting, and Hsing Yun was his chief guide. Ven. Zhu Yuan was the co-ordinator, Ven. Guang Ci the treasurer, and eight laymen also acted as leaders. All toured the island, most of them on foot, for 40 days, even visiting some of the islands, and preached to explain the sutras. Their activity roused great enthusiasm, and all was recorded in a diary.

In 1968 Hsing Yun decided on 16 July to start another islandwide tour of 24 days with his students from the Dong Fang seminary. The 30 public preaching events included choral singing, puppet shows and ventriloquism, as well as films. They were accompanied by two mobile vans with equipment, displayed thousands of posters, and distributed 3,000 booklets on the Buddha. In 1987, to celebrate the twentieth anniversary of FGS, there was a third such islandwide tour, which also included a mobile medical van and a basketball team; this time it also visited prisons.

From the beginning of his preaching career, Hsing Yun was expert at improvising in unusual venues rather than temples, and recruiting young volunteers locally to help, so as to reach wide audiences. In 1956 at his very first preaching event in Yilan, there were not enough seats, but people stood in the rain for two hours to listen and watch. He also preached in army bases, adapting to a style calculated to entertain soldiers.

An effect of his preaching in prisons was that the Ven. Ci Rong became Chief Probation Officer in a local court. Events at the national level have included preaching in Sun Yi Xian (or Sun Yat Sen) Memorial Hall and the National Art Museum; his programmes mostly include dancing and illuminations.[19]

---

19 The material taken from the 1987 Handbook ends here. The information in the next three paragraphs is more up to date, being derived from our own fieldwork.

FGS organizes all kinds of excursions, particularly pilgrimages, though these tend to offer touristic enjoyments too. In fact, FGS has its own travel agency. This organizes cruises, on which Buddhist ceremonies are performed; they have even hired a jet to visit the North Pole and see the Northern Lights. Participants are treated to new experiences (often with an American flavour) such as chicken nuggets – though these are Buddhist nuggets and so of course vegetarian.

In 2011 began an annual series of events called *Shenming Lianyi Hui*, 'Assemblies of the Deities of the World'. These are annual pilgrimages of a novel kind: all the deities in Taiwan, plus some from overseas, visit the Memorial Center to pay their respects to the Buddha, to acknowledge his suzerainty, and thus promote religious harmony in the whole island and beyond. An explicit aim is to bring believers in folk religions into Buddhism, but deities such as the Virgin Mary are also included. FGS claims that in 2016 world records were broken when 3,000 temples took part, bringing together 380,000 believers. Serving meals (usually referred to in English as 'banquets') to a thousand visitors at once has become commonplace.

Figure 4: Group of pilgrims at Gaoxiong, 25 December 2018

Hsing Yun's proselytizing has by no means been confined to public events. He has introduced Buddhist ritual and custom into the daily life of his followers. For instance, he has popularized Buddhist weddings, at which he has himself often officiated. (Buddhist funerals are of course traditionally of central importance, and FGS continues to run them, but they tend to receive less emphasis than weddings.) Similarly, he has turned birthdays, including his own, into lively occasions for Buddhist-flavoured celebration, and he organizes joint events for people sharing the same birthday. Other events for domestic celebration are also exploited for public celebration, sometimes even in the FGS HQ. Innovation has gone further: the Buddha Light International Association (BLIA) gives certificates and public recognition to families who are deemed to display Buddhist virtues in their daily lives.

Chapter 5

FGS AND EDUCATION[1]

Stuart Chandler has written that Master Hsing Yun's 'efforts have centred on creating joy through Buddhist education. ... Ultimate liberation from suffering can occur only through realizing the joy of the dharma, and providing people with this opportunity ... is the mission of Fo Guang Shan's multifaceted educational enterprises'.[2]

The Chinese Xinhai revolution of 1911 opened the door to educational reform for the Buddhist Saṅgha, though some seeds had been sown earlier: the Meiji Restoration in Japan gradually gave ideas to the Chinese on how to modernize by learning from the West, and in particular Hong Kong was full of Christian churches and street preachers. In his desire to overhaul Chinese Buddhism so that it contributed to the wellbeing of ordinary people, Tai Xu was vividly aware that the Saṅgha needed to be better educated. In his writings he argued that there should be fewer monks, but they should be properly trained; graduation from secondary education should be a prerequisite for ordination, and to become a Buddhist teacher should require at least 12 further years of monastic education. Monks should also learn maths, science and languages. At first he argued that they should do so by attending public schools alongside laymen, but then he founded a seminary on the east coast called Min Nan in which he radically revised syllabus and teaching methods. However, the chaotic conditions created by the Japanese invasion made it impossible for him to settle down in one place. The next generation realized some of his dreams, but he died in 1947.

By then, however, he had followers, and the most important of them turned out to be Hsing Yun, who had been taught and inspired by him.

---

1 For the information in this chapter we are heavily indebted to Dr Matthew Orsborn, aka Ven. Huifeng Shih.
2 Chandler, *Establishing a Pure Land on Earth*, p. 75. Chandler devotes a whole chapter to education, entitled 'Cultivating talent through education'.

In Chapter 4 we have given an account of his life until he fled to Taiwan in 1949 in the wake of Jiang Jie Shi and his GMD; he was in a group of monks who had organized themselves into a medical team. However, like many of them, he was destitute and almost friendless, and had a very hard time at first; he was even arrested on suspicion of being a communist spy. Finally, in 1952, through the help of a local abbot he met a rich businessman from Yilan, in northeastern Taiwan, who needed someone to run his local temple, Lei Yin, and offered him the post.

Hsing Yun made education the foundation of his movement

As soon as Hsing Yun moved to Yilan he began to proselytize. As he has written: '[Ever] since I started propagating the Dharma, I have been following the teachings of Master Tai Xu. Buddhism is not a religion of empty talk. We have to start by improving people's lives'.[3] He began to give lectures on Buddhism and would go to preach in unconventional places such as the night market. He founded a Buddhist chanting society, and the first known Buddhist choir. He held evening classes to help poor students acquire a basic education, and weekend classes for children in which he taught drawing and calligraphy. He became a residential monk of the temple in 1954. In 1959 he organized vast lantern parades on the Buddha's birthday all over Yilan, with the aim also of supporting Tibetan Buddhism when the Chinese were attacking Tibet; it is estimated that of the population of Yilan, which was 50,000 at the time, 30,000 took part. He edited and largely wrote Buddhist magazines, as well as weightier publications, and went round giving free copies to some and selling them to those who could afford to pay.

In 1967 he founded Fo Guang Shan near Gaoxiong in southern Taiwan. He founded it on some barren land which he bought with his own money (earned, he says, from royalties), and it is noteworthy that in the first institution he set up there was not a monastery but a seminary.

As we have shown in a previous article,[4] Hsing Yun at first arranged for some of his leading disciples to go to study in Japan and there acquire university degrees, even up to a doctorate; some of the other eminent monks and nuns in Taiwan in this period did the same. Hsing

---

3 Quoted by us in Yao and Gombrich, 'Christianity as model and analogue', p. 214.
4 Yao and Gombrich, 'Telescope and microscope', pp. 135–38.

Yun himself, however, did not wish to follow suit (perhaps he felt he could not absent himself from his ministry in Taiwan for so long), and he turned his energies to providing both religious and more general education in Taiwan, both for his disciples and for the general public.

Figure 5: Grand Master Hsing Yun tonsures a Western novice at FGS, 2014

The personnel

The original seminary, for males, is now the women's college, the men having moved to a new building. The aim of the seminaries is to train monastics. They also award BA degrees, but these are not recognized by the government. Since Hsing Yun opened this first seminary, many other monasteries in Taiwan have gone down the same road, but to meet the cost of a seminary is beyond the means of the smaller monasteries. About three-quarters of the FGS monks and nuns have been trained in an FGS seminary.

We mention the training of novices below. With a few exceptions, the other pupils are aged 18 to 35, and the ratio of women to men is about ten to one; they are all unmarried and hardly any have been divorced. Those who come from monasteries allied to FGS retain their affiliation. Many of those who enter the seminary are laity who intend to ordain in due course, and some have been ordained elsewhere. Some entrants are considerably older than most of the other students; their experience of life is taken into account, and they often end up in administrative roles.

The FGS college/seminary system has trained vast numbers of monastics in Taiwan and other countries. At first most pupils were local or from China; then they came from Malaysia, Hong Kong and Singapore; recently there have been many Chinese from the USA and Australia. Ninety-eight per cent of the students are Chinese.

Most of the teachers for religious subjects such as liturgy and doctrine are from the same lineage as Hsing Yun. Some of the teachers for Buddhist doctrine are laity, and there is no prejudice against lay teachers. In graduate studies, which play only a very minor part in the whole system (see below), the teachers are lay academics.

Content of the education

In contrast to the movement as a whole (see Chapter 2) the FGS training for monastics follows the Chan tradition and emphasizes meditation; other features of the daily routine are chanting and cleaning. Like most Chinese Buddhist institutions, the seminaries follow the Dharmaguptaka *Vinaya*; learning *vinaya* includes all the rituals and the relevant prostrations. There are retreats, typically lasting seven days, one in the winter and two in the summer; of these, one is open to anyone, the other two are stricter. For the retreats, males take the full novice ordination, but women take only *śikṣamāṇā* ordination[5] so do not get shaved. At the end of a retreat most participants disrobe and 'give back' the precepts, but a minority do not because they have decided to make a long-term commitment.

Ordination is normally lifelong; to leave is humiliating. Your preceptor is an abbot or abbess, but for the most part that is a formality: it is often your teachers who decide whether you are fit to be ordained. Unlike in early Buddhism and Theravāda there are three levels of ordination for men, not just two; the lowest level has been divided into two. The first Chinese level, tonsure, is a brief ceremony in which no precepts are taken; but the monk who shaves (tonsures) you remains your master for life – one could say that he is your 'father

---

5 This is a stage, already created in ancient times, which is preliminary to becoming a novice. The word *śikṣamāṇā* means 'trainee'. There is no close equivalent for males, but for them too there is now a stage preliminary to the novitiate – see next paragraph.

in religion' – and this is what determines your monastic lineage.⁶ At tonsure you get a new name and live in quarters separated from the laity, and expectations of your behaviour are higher. You take the precepts of a novitiate an indeterminate time later, and this may be at a different institution and/or with a different preceptor. A full/higher ordination, to become a monk or nun in the full sense, is known as a 'triple platform', because the three levels of ordination are conferred within one ceremony, which lasts several weeks.⁷ These are large events with at least a hundred candidates and sometimes many more. The ordinations must be conferred by ten monks (for both sexes) and ten nuns (for the females), and many support staff are needed, so only the biggest monasteries can stage them, and even these only take place once in four years at the most. FGS higher ordinations waver between the Yogācāra precepts and those in the Mahāyāna *Brahmajāla Sūtra*.⁸ One may continue to study even after taking full ordination; presumably this is linked to the fact that in FGS educational qualifications play a major part in monastic ranking.⁹

In addition to the monastic discipline, all male pupils receive Taiwanese military training, even if that impinges on their studies, and there are military rewards and punishments.

As for the academic aspect: the courses last two to four years (though those who arrive already well qualified are allowed to graduate sooner). In Appendix 1 below, we give a curriculum for a full course.

Education beyond the seminary

Hsing Yun gives unremitting attention to education of virtually every kind, and we should mention other formal institutions that FGS has set up. It has founded two universities in Taiwan and three abroad, one in California, one in Australia and one in the Philippines. Despite international rhetoric, there has been little success in getting into US higher education.

---

6 For an excellent account of tonsure (with photographs) and its significance, see Welch, *The Practice of Chinese Buddhism*, pp. 247 and 269–76.

7 These ordinations are described and explained by Welch, *The Practice of Chinese Buddhism*, pp. 285–94.

8 This is a completely different text from the *Brahmajāla Sutta* which is the first sutta in the *Dīgha Nikāya* of the Pali Canon.

9 For details see Yao and Gombrich, 'Telescope and microscope', pp. 141 and 149–50.

As with seminaries, Buddhist monasteries in Taiwan have competed in founding universities, which are secular institutions. Some of these universities confer higher degrees (MA, a few even PhD) and a small number also have what they call 'research institutes', but the standards in research do not command wide recognition. In 2012 one of the FGS universities, Fo Guang University, started a 'Buddhist research institute', but as we have already mentioned in Chapter 2, when Hsing Yun came to open it he said in his speech that doing new research on Buddhism should not be given a high priority.[10] One may surmise that, like many people, he assumes that nothing of importance about Buddhism remains to be discovered; and indeed what passes for education in many Buddhist monasteries can give that impression.

Nor has HY neglected informal and part-time education, both traditional and innovative. For instance, he has encouraged the formation of Buddhist reading clubs. A novel aspect of his educational efforts is that he encourages people to come and live in an FGS monastery for as long as they like with no commitment to becoming ordained. What counts, in his eyes, is to give everyone maximal opportunities to get involved with Buddhism.

At the other end of the age scale, Hsing Yun has also founded kindergartens and primary schools. He has stressed that it is important to teach children good behaviour while they are very young. Though Tai Xu envisaged that novices could be trained in lay schools, this was found not to work well, so they now have their own programmes inside the seminaries; the pupils are aged 12 to 18, and the courses follow government requirements for that age group. Similarly, he has founded programmes for BLIA scouts.

In the People's Republic of China FGS has built a Buddhist library in Jindu, Hsing Yun's home town, and has a 50-year management contract for it.

Education a vehicle for Confucian values

As Chandler has written, '[T]he Master has always regarded a systematized, comprehensive education, especially of the Saṅgha, to be the key to the regeneration of society and the revival of Buddhism'.[11] In this, as in so much else, he has been a devoted disciple of Tai Xu.

---

10 Reported to us at the time by a colleague who was present.
11 Chandler, *Establishing a Pure Land on Earth*, p. 118.

Tai Xu cared passionately about raising the educational standards of all Chinese Buddhists, but he naturally concentrated his efforts on educating the Saṅgha, in the hope that they would in turn educate the rest of the Buddhist population. Moreover, conditions were so bad that he always had the greatest trouble in raising money. Hsing Yun, while he began his career amidst poverty and hardship, came to work in a peaceful and relatively stable society, which enabled him to found educational institutions of all kinds. The attitude underlying this might be called Confucian paternalism.

Taiwan, historically a part of China, remains fundamentally a Confucian society. Confucianism teaches that it is the collective which demands our total allegiance, and the concerns of the individual must always be subordinated to the concerns of the larger unit – ultimately to the welfare of the whole of Chinese society. How the welfare of society is determined and how it can be attained is to be decided by a hierarchy of authority. Throughout society the model for this hierarchy is supplied by the patriarchal family. The details of how all this is carried out are supplied by the bureaucracy, a form of organization which China has bequeathed to the world.

Hsing Yun has found it easy to appreciate the straightforward hierarchy and authoritarianism of the Roman Catholic church, and to institutionalize it in Fo Guang Shan, where it is applied with the bureaucratic rigour which assures the authorities and the local public that this institution follows the best tradition of administration. Within the FGS Saṅgha there are eight named ranks with many more scales, and an elaborate code for promotion. Many criteria contribute to ranking, but the most important is educational attainment. The certified qualifications which entitle monks and nuns to hold office are the educational qualifications in Buddhist studies earned at the movement's own colleges. This overwhelming emphasis on formal education is the legacy of Tai Xu; but perhaps even Tai Xu would have been surprised by the degree to which written academic examinations serve the purpose of establishing the monastic hierarchy. The model for this feature is presumably the traditional practice of the Chinese government.

While a complex hierarchy of ranks and offices was traditional in large Chinese monasteries, probably the only features of the FGS administration which distinguish it from the traditional monastic norm are this emphasis on formal education as the paramount qualification, and the very large role given in the hierarchy to nuns.[12]

---

12 *FGS 20th Yearbook*, 1987, pp. 38-40.

If we look at the summit of this hierarchy, the authority wielded by the movement's founder is of course charismatic, as against traditional or rational/bureaucratic. This status is symbolized by the fact that Hsing Yun resigned as abbot of the main monastery in 1992,[13] when he founded the BLIA, and since then has floated in the stratosphere above all who hold designated positions.

Though he is over 90, and alas blind, until now Hsing Yun has had more complete control over his church than the Pope has over Roman Catholics. This is not considered remarkable, since it stands in the general Chinese tradition of the autocratic 'master'. Hsing Yun recognizes that his position is comparable to that of the Pope. He has visited Pope John Paul II, and used to cultivate a relationship, both in public and in private, with the Roman Catholic Archbishop of Taiwan, the late Paul Shan Kuo-Hsi, SJ. He sees his monastic disciples as comparable to Roman Catholic priests and nuns, whose calling should bring them into constant involvement with the laity. Influenced by both Confucianism and Roman Catholicism, he thus preserves the Buddhist tradition of the special status of the Saṅgha, while showing them how to adapt to a more secular world.

Figure 6: The two incumbent nuns give a sermon at Yongjing, a branch of BLIA

---

13 The Buddha Light International Association (BLIA), the lay counterpart to FGS, was founded in 1991 at a ceremony in Taipei. The eminent KMT politician, Wu Boxiung, has long been its Honorary Chairman. See Yao and Gombrich, 'Telescope and microscope', pp. 143–44.

Appendices

Appendix 1: Curriculum of FGS Buddhist College (2018)

Course Code	English Course Title	Course Type	Credits	Notes
BU14A	Introduction to Buddhist Studies (I)	Required	2	Full Academic Year
BU12A	History of Indian Buddhism (I)	Required	2	Full Academic Year
BU15A	Guided Reading on Buddhist Scriptures (I)	Required	2	Full Academic Year
BU107	Seven Day Retreat on Recitation of the Buddha's Name	Required	1	
BU115	Buddhist Comportment (I)	Required	0	Full Academic Year
BU141	Introduction to Buddhist Scriptures	Required	3	
GE111	Chinese (I)	Required	3	
GE121	English (I)	Required	3	
GE140	Informatics and Internet	Required	3	
GE151	Physical Education (I)	Required	0	
GE161	General Education (I)	Required	0	
GE510	The Age of Exploration and the Formation of the Modern World	Elective	3	Must select one of four core curriculum courses during first and second semesters of the first year.
GE520	World Cultural Heritage	Elective	3	
GE530	From Homer to Dante	Elective	3	
GE540	World Arts and the Construction of Civilization	Elective	3	
BU15B	Guided Reading of Buddhist Scriptures (II)	Required	2	Full Academic Year
BU115	Buddhist Comportment (II)	Required	0	Full Academic Year
BU122	Seven Day Retreat for Meditation	Required	1	
BU14B	Introduction Studies (II) to Buddhist	Required	2	Full Academic Year

Course Code	English Course Title	Course Type	Credits	Notes
BU12B	History Buddhism (II) of India	Required	2	Full Academic Year
BU142	Lucid Introduction to the *One Hundred Dharmas*	Elective	3	
BU144	Basic Issues in Buddhism	Elective	3	
BU145	*Pañcaskandha-prakarana* (in Chinese)	Elective	3	
GE112	Chinese (II)	Required	3	
GE122	English (II)	Required	3	
GE130	Mathematics	Required	3	
GE152	Physical Education (II)	Required	0	
GE162	General Education (II)	Required	0	
GE510	The Age of Exploration and the Formation of the Modern World	Elective	3	Must select one of four core curriculum courses during the first and second semesters of the first year.
GE520	World Cultural Heritage	Elective	3	
GE530	From Homer to Dante	Elective	3	
GE540	World Arts and the Construction of Civilization	Elective	3	
BU230	Organization of Buddhist recitation	Required	1	
BU231	Monastic Lexicon	Required	1	
BU22A	History of Chinese Buddhism (I)	Required	2	Full Academic Year
BU255	History of Theravāda Buddhism	Elective	3	
BU233	Buddhist English	Required	3	
BU256	Buddhist Iconography	Elective	3	
BU304	1st year Sanskrit I	Core Elective	3	
BU305	1st year Pali I		3	
BU306	1st year Tibetan I		3	
BU235	Selective Readings of Mahāyāna Texts	Elective	3	

Course Code	English Course Title	Course Type	Credits	Notes
BU254	Buddhist Images and Computer Graphics	Elective	3	
BU236	The Language of Chinese Buddhist Texts	Elective	3	
GE430	Ecology and Biodiversity	Elective	3	Must select one of four core curriculum courses during the first and second semesters of the second year.
GE440	Earth Sciences	Elective	3	
GE460	History of Science Development	Elective	3	
GE420	Psychology	Elective	3	
GE320	Principles of Economics	Elective	3	
GE330	Introduction to Legal Science	Elective	3	Must select one of four core curriculum courses during the first and second semesters of the second year.
GE340	Social Principles	Elective	3	
GE350	Organization and Management	Elective	3	
GE153	Physical Education (IIV)	Required	0	
BU241	Organization of Meditation Retreat	Required	1	
BU242	Lexicon of Chan Buddhism	Required	1	
BU22B	History of Chinese Buddhism (II)	Required	2	Full Academic Year
BU257	History of Tibetan Buddhism	Elective	3	
BU258	History of Taiwanese Buddhism	Required	2	
BU259	English Translation of Buddhist Scriptures	Elective	3	
BU304	1st year Sanskrit II	Core Elective	3	
BU305	1st year Pali II		3	
BU306	1st year Tibetan II		3	
BU248	Introduction to Buddhist Sects	Elective	3	
BU249	Chinese Buddhist Art	Elective	3	
BU251	Translation of Buddhist Terminology	Elective	3	

Course Code	English Course Title	Course Type	Credits	Notes
BU252	Readings of English articles on Primary Concepts in Buddhism	Elective	3	
BU253	Guided Reading on the Lotus Sutra	Elective	3	
BU256	Buddhist Iconography	Elective	3	
BU254	Buddhist Images and Computer Graphics	Elective	3	
GE430	Ecology and Biodiversity	Elective	3	Must select one of four core curriculum courses during the first and second semesters of the second year.
GE440	Earth Sciences	Elective	3	
GE460	History of Science Development	Elective	3	
GE420	Psychology	Elective	3	
GE320	Principles of Economics	Elective	3	
GE330	Introduction to Legal Science	Elective	3	Must select one of four core curriculum courses during the first and second semesters of the second year.
GE340	Social Principles		3	
GE350	Organization and Management	Elective	3	
GE154	Physical Education (IIV)	Elective	0	
BU310	Buddhist Ritual and Liturgy	Required	2	
BU307	2nd year Sanskrit I	Core Elective	3	
BU308	2nd year Pali I		3	
BU309	2nd year Tibetan I		3	
BU314	Research on Tiantai School	Core Elective	3	Must select two of five.
BU315	Research on Huayan School		3	
BU316	Research on Chan School		3	
BU317	Research on Pure Land Buddhism		3	
BU318	Research on Yogācāra School		3	
BU319	Foguang Studies	Elective	3	

Course Code	English Course Title	Course Type	Credits	Notes
BU320	Japanese-Korean Buddhism	Elective	3	
BU340	Topical Studies of Buddhist Philosophy	Elective	3	
BU341	Precious Teachings among Chan Buddhist Temples: Administration and Regulation	Elective	3	
BU302	Religious Law and Policy	Elective	3	
BU344	Philosophy of Prajnaparamita	Elective	3	
BU345	Research on Sino-Tibetan Buddhist Studies	Elective	3	
BU351	Bachelor Studies for Graduation (I)	Required	3	
BU327	Buddhist Missiology	Required	2	
BU307	2nd year Sanskrit	Core Elective	3	
BU308	2nd year Pali		3	
BU309	2nd year Tibetan		3	
BU335	Buddhist Historiography	Elective	3	
BU336	Selective Readings in Buddhist Literature	Elective	3	
BU337	Buddhist Logic	Elective	3	
BU342	Sino-Indian Cultural History	Elective	3	
BU343	The Demonstration of Consciousness Only	Elective	3	
BU349	Advanced Buddhist Japanese	Elective	3	
BU350	Guided Reading of *Avataṃsaka* Sutra	Elective	2	
BU410	Practice of Saṅgha Ministry	Required	2	
BU224	Buddhist Ethics	Elective	3	
BU325	Readings on English Buddhist Works	Elective	3	
BU412	American Buddhism	Elective	3	

Course Code	English Course Title	Course Type	Credits	Notes
BU414	Topics of Madhyamika Philosophy	Elective	3	
BU434	Bachelor Studies for Graduation (II)	Required	3	
BU432	Buddhism in Contemporary Taiwan Society	Elective	3	
BU433	Buddhist Hagiography	Elective	3	

Appendix 2: Educational background of FGS monastics, recorded in the *20th Yearbook*

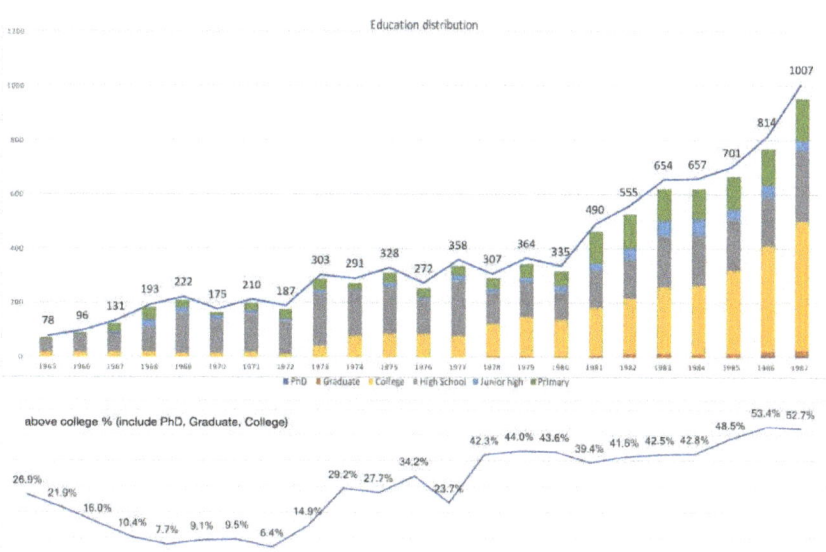

Chapter 6

PUBLIC RITUAL AT FGS MAIN MONASTERY, GAOXIONG[1]

A *fahui* (Dharma assembly) is a ritual of worship for a god or other superhuman figure – in Buddhism usually a Buddha or bodhisattva. In FGS monastics are always present. Certain *fahui* are performed at FGS's main monastery annually or on other fixed dates (typically reckoned by the lunar calendar), and a list of them is kept.

Since 1971 there have been annual *fahui* to Kuan Yin: 19 February celebrates her birth, 19 June her Enlightenment and 19 September her renunciation. (These are lunar dates.) In 1971 about 7,000 people attended; since c.1987, attendance has been more like 10,000, with many taking the Refuges. There is a large ceremony of chanting the *Avataṃsaka Sūtra*, to which the *Sūtra of Great Compassion* has recently been added. This *fahui* is also held in the branch temples and is accompanied by many miracles.

On 9 January the birthday of the Jade Emperor (*Gong Fo Zhai Tien*) is celebrated with a vegetarian feast to thank the Emperor and his attendant gods for their hard work over the past year. On this day the Jade Emperor and his relatives all became Buddhists and patrons of Buddhism. On the eve (8 January) FGS invites the Buddha with the Jade Emperor and the gods to this feast. The Three Jewels are invited too.[2] All night there are offerings of flowers, incense, etc. in a grand ceremony. In 1987 Kuala Lumpur's Temple of Heaven's Empress invited FGS to perform this ritual.

---

1 This chapter is based almost entirely on pp. 351ff. of the 1987 *FGS Yearbook*.
2 The Buddha is invited in the form of a statue; the Dharma in the form of a scripture or a Chinese character for the word 'Dharma'; the Saṅgha in the form of the monastics present.

The Buddha's birthday (*Yu Fo*) is on 8 April; a small image of the Buddha is bathed. In 1999 Shen Zhi-Hui, a Buddhist legislator, led 207 members of the legislature in proposing that the Buddha's birthday be celebrated as a national holiday in the second week of May (lunar) together with Mothers' Day. On 31 August that year the President, Li Den-Hui, came to FGS to celebrate Hsing Yun's birthday, and announced that 8 April would henceforth be nationally celebrated as the Buddha's birthday.[3] The government has ruled that on this day all killing is strictly forbidden. Since 1981, when the FGS Great Shrine was completed, there has been a three-day talent competition for kindergarten pupils. At the Gate of Non-Duality there is a fair, and sometimes also a book fair, and all FGS branches hold fairs too. In 1987 the date coincided with an FGS alms round led by Hsing Yun. For three days there were ceremonies, starting at 11 a.m. at the Main Shrine and ending at 7 p.m. with evening chanting. On 10 April in the morning the Three Refuges were taken in the Great Compassion Hall; this was followed by the release of captive animals.

Qing Men Fa Hui normally falls in April; this is a *fahui* for ancestors and for celebrating filial piety, and Hsing Yun preaches on filial piety (on which he has also published a book). At the Gaoxiong monastery Hsing Yun has also had a pillar erected for the dead and all day someone is there chanting prayers. The bodhisattva Kṣitigarbha resides in all such pillars and helps the dead.

On 15 July there is the Avalambana Basin assembly (*Obon*), the service to feed the hungry ghosts (see note 5). It is also the end of the monastic summer rains retreat.[4] Hsing Yun says that on this day one must not kill animals (as had been customary) but instead save lives and transfer the merit to those in hell, including soldiers killed in wars. In 1976 FGS held the Obon at its HQ at the shrine of Kṣitigarbha.

The birthday of Bhaiṣajyaguru is on 29 September. Both the HQ and the branch temples hold three to seven days of *sutra* chanting. In 1964 the devotees in Shou Shan temple were chanting his name so fervently that relics came out of the candles.

---

3 Hsing Yun has said that 8 April should be known as the Buddha's day, 8 December as Dharma day (because that was the day of the Buddha's Enlightenment), and 16 July as Saṅgha day (because on that day the Saṅgha make their offering to the Buddha). This is on p. 333 of the 1987 *FGS Yearbook*.

4 This corresponds to the Indian *vassa*, the rains retreat, though in China and Taiwan there is no rainy season.

86   Chinese Buddhism Today

Amitābha's birthday is on 17 November. Ever since Hsing Yun has lived in Yilan, FGS has held seven days of chanting.

The *fahui* of transmitting precepts (*Chuan jie fa hui*)

In 1971 when the Great Compassion Shrine was completed, a ceremony was held to give the five precepts and the Bodhisattva precepts to the laity. In 1986 FGS decided to have two such annual ceremonies, one in the spring and one in the autumn. In 1977, to mark the tenth anniversary of the FGS, they had three platforms for the Saṅgha as well as the five precepts and the Bodhisattva precepts for the laity. 500 Saṅgha members and 1500 laity took vows. Hsing Yun was Master of Precepts, Zhen Hua was Master of Ritual, Zhu Yuan was Master of Demeanour.

Special occasional rituals of FGS

Wan Yuan Shue Lou Fa Hui （萬緣水陸法會）**'Ritual of Water and Land ceremony of universal *paccaya* (causal relationship)'**[5]

---

5   This is the same as the Great Repentance of the Emperor Liang, which we have mentioned in Yao and Gombrich, 'Christianity as model and analogue', pp. 230–31, but on a far larger scale. The latter requires the participation of only five Saṅgha members and so can be performed by branch temples. Water and Land requires 50 to 100 monastics. The content of the two ceremonies may overlap considerably. The main text chanted can be the *Bhaiṣajyaguru* (Medicine Buddha) sutra; cf. 29 September entry above. Water and Land is called *paccaya*, because this alludes to the Buddhist teaching that everything is related, so that this huge ceremony is effective on a cosmic scale. The content can also overlap with that of *Obon* (its Japanese name), mentioned above, which can also be called Great Compassion. It can include any or all of the other rituals, and FGS claims to specialize in holding it on a grand scale. Welch avoids settling for any of these names but refers to them as 'plenary mass'. He describes the origin of the Water Penance (*Shui-ch'an*) (*The Practice of Chinese Buddhism*, p. 188), and then writes; 'The purpose of the plenary mass was to save all the souls of the dead on land and sea (hence the term *shui-lu*)' (p. 190). An important difference is that it is generally felt that Obon is performed particularly for one's own kin.

Figure 7: Opening of a Water and Land ritual, Kuala Lumpur, Malaysia, 11 February 2018

In 1973, after the 18 April solar calendar, Hsing Yun wrote:

> China is taken by the Communists. Our motherland is now a hell. Millions of people are suffering: friends and relatives, including soldiers. Filial piety is no longer practised, no rituals are performed, morality has declined, everyone is angry and cruel, society is full of wounds and scars. Can there be more suffering than this? So on 16 March lunar calendar I wanted to perform a ritual of *Ching ming* for seven days to repay all parents with the ritual of water and land, to promote the virtues of Chinese culture and reconfirm filial piety. This will benefit those drowned in the river [of *saṃsāra*], and ghosts and evil spirits, and eliminate the bad karma of donors and create a harmonious society. I have asked a superior elder, the retired abbot of Shen qi sha temple, Hong Kong, Ven Ming Chang, with hundreds of pure monks and nuns, to chant in order to save soldiers and civilians killed in wars, as well as our ancestors back for several generations, and spirits wandering in the ten directions with no one to perform rites on their behalf. We can release all these from suffering and carry them across the river. The merit of this ceremony will be transferred to create prosperity in the country, make people happy, produce a good climate, and make universal peace. So I pray all the dharma

protectors to come to FGS and join in our worship and share our dharma happiness.

On 14–16 November 1975 a three-day ceremony was held which included the inauguration of the Escort Buddha by opening its eyes, laying the foundation of the main shrine, and marking the completion of the male seminary. It was attended by an audience of 100,000, and HY inaugurated it with a purification. Mañjuśrī was installed in a shrine called *Da Zhi Dian*. There was an exhibition of Buddhist objects; a ceremony of chanting the Medicine Sutra in the shrine of Bhaiṣajyaguru; and a ceremony of chanting the sutra of Water and Land in the Shrine of Memory, with loud dharma singing by the general public. Then from 10 a.m. on the final day (16 November) Hsing Yun led hundreds of Saṅgha members in performing elaborate ceremonies. He wrote a poem for the occasion in which he declared that the sand and stone came from Gaoxiong and Pingdong, and the water from Xi Lai (in California); the effort of all Taiwanese had created the largest Buddha statue in Taiwan. There was a banquet for a thousand tables, and he declared that the Water and Land ceremony would be an annual event.

On 2–4 December, the Water and Land ritual was held from 10 a.m. to 8 p.m., in two ceremonies, one in Da zhi dian for the living, the other in the Hall of Memory for the dead. It culminated in a transfer of merit in the Great Compassion Hall. A total of 480 small Escort Buddhas were inaugurated.

The year 1977 was the tenth anniversary of FGS, and a seven-day Water and Land ceremony began on 19 November. More than 100 monastics took part. There were seven platforms of chanting: the inner platform in the Shrine of Compassion; the large platform; the Hua Yen platform; the platform of all other sutras; the platform of Medicine; the platform of the Pure Land; the platform of the Lotus Sutra. Then at 20.30 p.m. Hsing Yun performed the purification. The next day at 4.30 a.m. all platforms began the seven-day chanting ceremony.

In 1978 the ceremony described in the previous paragraph was repeated, but on a smaller scale.

In 1986 FGS repeated the ceremony of Water and Land, which they reckoned to be their fourth, on 15–21 November. Again there were seven platforms: the inner platform was in the main shrine = Da xuang bao dian (大雄寶殿); the large platform in the Shrine of Great Compassion; the Hua Yen, Lotus, other sutras and the Medicine Sutra were chanted in the male and female seminaries; the Pure Land platform, in the

Meditation Hall, was the biggest and most decorated shrine. Chanting began on the morning of the 16th, and there was an earthquake, which was taken as an auspicious response. On the 17th it was raining, and this too was taken to be auspicious.

Since the 1980s, FGS at New Year has held 30 days of peaceful lantern celebration. Lighted lanterns are placed in the mountains to suggest the radiation of the Buddha's light. People are thus awoken to leave the delusions of life and create a happy and beneficial (*le li*) society; everyone receives the Buddha's merit. FGS also puts on automatic (electric) lantern shows, and the monastery is lit up like a lantern city. Each year FGS lights at least 100,000 lanterns for the lunar month of January.

Jiang Jie Shi died on 5 April (solar) 1975. On the initiative of BAROC[6] the anniversary is celebrated with a three-day ceremony, in the hope that he will be reborn in the Pure Land and then return to earth.

'Transmission of Dharma' *Chuan fa da dian* (傳法大典)

On 22 September 1985, Hsing Yun insisted on resigning as abbot. The ceremony began at 10 a.m. in the main shrine with drums and bells. Among the thousands of disciples present were the Chairman of the Guo Min Dang, the mayor of Gaoxiong, and men who had been ordained with Hsing Yun in Qi Xia Shan in China, who were thus the fifth generation of Qi Xia and also the 48th generation of Lin Ji.

The Ven. Wu Yi was there as a witness, and to install Ven. Xin Ping as the second abbot. Hsing Yun led a musical procession, and on arrival he read the dharma scroll and passed it to Xin Ping. He also gave him a rope and a bowl, and a written code of conduct, 'the eye of the Dharma'. Xin bowed to Hsing Yun nine times and vowed to take the latter's wish as his own, to preach to benefit society, and to receive guests from the ten directions. Ven. Yue Ji, a senior monk, spoke to exhort Xin Ping. Hsing Yun then spoke: he had resigned for four reasons:

(1) To show that Dharma principle is more important than human principle.

---

6 BAROC is the Buddhist Association of the Republic of China. Jiang Jie Shi brought it with him when he fled to Taiwan in 1949. Until the end of the dictatorship in 1989, all ordination in Taiwan had to be performed by and registered with BAROC.

90   *Chinese Buddhism Today*

(2) There was nothing that was required to be done by him personally.
(3) Resignation was not retirement.
(4) This enhanced the exchange between the generations.

Hsing Yun also chose to transmit the 49th generation of Lin Ji to 30 of his disciples, who came from Taiwan, USA, Canada, Thailand, Malaysia, Indonesia, Korea and Hong Kong.

In December 1986 at FGS headquarters, FGS held a recitation of sutras and tantras headed by Tibetan and Han Buddhist senior masters to pray for world peace. They received greetings from the Thai royal family and Taiwanese politicians. Hsing Yun organized it in his capacity as head of the Han and Tibetan cultural association, a position he relinquished when he realized that Tantriks ate meat and did not practise celibacy.

In 1987, on the 20th anniversary of FGS, on 5 April a collective island-wide begging round began at 8 a.m. It had four principles:

(1) To follow both the Buddha's teachings and the model of Xuan Zang, who travelled on foot and maintained an ascetic lifestyle.
(2) To commemorate Jiang Jie Shi.
(3) To commemorate the Yellow Emperor and those who died in founding the Republic and in subsequent wars, and all the ancestors of the Chinese race.
(4) To wish the nation power, energy and prosperity. This has four meanings: 1. Work to create the nation's prosperity. 2. Make Buddhism flourish. 3. Create brightness in the human world. 4. Make Buddhists believe in His righteous teachings.

Abbot Xin Ping added that we have to train people to work hard.

At 9.30 a.m. began a parade with the national flag and 20 Buddhist flags. Xin Ping marched at the head of 108 monastics wearing bamboo hats, grey robes, with a coffee-coloured robe on top. In one hand each held a walking stick, in the other a bowl. They marched 60 km from north to south, arriving at the gate of FGS at 10 a.m. on 6 May – the Buddha's birthday.

Hsing Yun came back from America to see it but did not take part. In Xi Lai he had been celebrating the Buddha's birthday with 2000 guests, including US politicians and officials. He made a speech saying that FGS is following early Buddhist teaching by going begging. This practice cultivates strength and endurance. It also avoids the killing of animals. (In the bowls they accept only money, not food. Mobile kitchens and accommodation precede the processions.) The donations were to go towards education and other charitable purposes. Businesses along the way displayed flowers, Buddha images, etc to welcome the participants. Buddhism was thus communicating with the general public. In two days' time the King of Thailand would have his 60th birthday and he, Hsing Yun, was invited; he would show the Thai people a video of this begging event.

On 13–14 September 1987 there was a ceremony for the 20th anniversary of FGS, combined with a ceremony of repaying one's debt to one's parents, and of the birthday of Hsing Yun. FGS invited anyone over 60 to come to their HQ. Hsing Yun wanted to celebrate his birthday not individually but in company with all those born in the same year as he was, or earlier, and to use this occasion to repay debts to all parents.

It began at 8 a.m. on the 13th with chanting the Medicine Sutra.

> 9.30 a.m.: collective graduation ceremony for all seminaries of FGS.
>
> 11 a.m.: award ceremony for FGS literature and photography.
>
> 2 p.m.: circus in main shrine for 800 'birthday' celebrants, with a fair, in which Hsing Yun went shopping to great applause.
>
> 6.30 p.m.: dinner for birthday celebrants, with dancing by high school and kindergarten students, and choirs from branch temples. Fireworks at the Gate of Non-Duality.
>
> 9 p.m.: devotees start from the Gate of Non-Duality and prostrate themselves every three steps as far as the main shrine.
>
> Next day (14th) 6 a.m.: a tonsure ceremony held by Hsing Yun, and three Refuges in the main shrine.
>
> 10.30 a.m.: party with dancing and singing for birthday celebrants, with the wish to make Taiwan prosperous and happy.

'Assembly of lay disciples'

The Assembly of lay disciples was first held in 1972 and became an annual event from 1975. It was originally held in the summer, but then moved to spring, and is still held today. The laity receive an account of what has been done in the past year and what is planned for the following year. Devotees wear sashes to show where they are from. In 1977 this event included a tonsure ceremony.

Appendix

Activities held in HQ from January to March 2015 (from Hsing Yun's calendar/diary)

Date (Western Calendar)	Contents	Department/Office
01/01	Buddhist weddings and announcement of the families with Three Goodnesses[1]	BLIA
01/01-07/01	Seven-day retreat[2]	Jingye Lin (office of the Pure Land)
01/01-18/01	Exhibition of imperial Official Exams in Taiwan[3]	Buddha Memorial Centre
01/01-01/02	Exhibition of oil paintings by former mayor	Buddha Memorial Centre
01/01-25/02	Exhibition of modern Taiwanese artists	Buddha Memorial Centre
01/01-22/03	Exhibition of Wedding Dresses	Buddha Memorial Centre
03/01-04/01	Chanting (two days)	Jingye Lin (office of the Pure Land)
04/01	Water Repentance Ritual[4]	Wan Shou Yuan (funeral parlour)
9/01-11/01	Camp for Cultivation of the Three Goodnesses (for FGS high school)	Voluntary team
10/01-29/03	Art exhibitions	FGS Gallery
10/01-29/03	Exhibition of cartoons on the Heart Sutra and the Sutra of the Sixth Patriarch[5]	Treasure Hall
17/01-22/02	Wooden puppet exhibition	Buddha Memorial Centre

---

1 The three goodnesses are to have a good heart, do good deeds, and speak kindly. The families have been nominated for this honour by their branches, and they are given a certificate. The event is run by the head of BLIA, a monk.
2 The retreat is a meditation for adults, of both sexes, led by a monk or nun. Dept of Pure Land organizes meditation, lectures, pilgrimages, etc. Founded 1997 to meet lay demand. The organizers are all clergy.
3 The imperial exams took place in pre-modern China. This is a historical exhibition. Taiwanese took the exams before the Japanese occupied Taiwan.
4 Chanting by monastics of the Water Repentance Sutra, composed by Wu Da in the Tang Dynasty, in the funeral parlour, which is staffed mainly by nuns.
5 The drawings show stories connected to the sutras.

Date (Western Calendar)	Contents	Department/Office
24/01	Seminar on Humanistic Buddhism	Humanistic Buddhism Study Club
24/01–25/01	Sutra copying	Sutra copying Hall
25/01	Great Compassion Repentance Ritual	Office for devotee guidance
27/01	Day of Dharma treasure (Fabao Jie), celebrated by giving vegetarian congee[6]	Dujian Yuan (Office of Supervision)
30/01–03/02	Retreat for teachers	BLIA
01/02	Water Repentance Ritual	Wan Shou Yuan (funeral parlour)
01/02	Marathon in Gaoxiong	Dujian Yuan (Office of Supervision)
1/2–7/2	Short-term Saṅgha[7]	FGS seminary
1/2–7/2	Seven-day Retreat	Jingye Lin (office of the Pure Land)
1/2–31/3	Circus from Shandong, New Year performances	Buddha Memorial Centre
4/2–6/2	Youth training camp teaching the value of life	Great Compassion Orphanage
6/2–8/2	Two-day chanting	Jingye Lin (office of the Pure Land)
6/2–8/2	18th session of youth volunteer training	FGS volunteers
6/2–10/2	Children's camp of life education	Great Compassion Orphanage
14/2–22/3	Exhibition of Shanghai folk paintings	Buddha Memorial Centre
18/2–20/2	Chinese New Year for foreigners	Humanistic Buddhism Research Centre
18/2–23/2	Trips in Taiwan	Youth of BLIA
19/2–23/2	New Year Dharma chanting	Wan Shou Yuan (funeral parlour)
19/2–15/3	Telling New Year stories	FGS Cultural Foundation
19/2–19/3	New Year Lanterns in Gaoxiong	Dujian Yuan (Office of Supervision)

---

6 Saṅgha gives porridge to the public to celebrate the Enlightenment of Shakyamuni (anniversary of Enlightenment: 8th December in lunar calendar).

7 Laity get ordained and live as a monastic for a week at the HQ, very popular!

Date (Western Calendar)	Contents	Department/Office
1/3–7/3	Seven-day retreat	Jingye Lin (office of the Pure Land)
6/3–7/3	Two-day chanting	Jingye Lin (office of the Pure Land)
6/3–19/3	Chinese opera	Buddha Memorial Centre
8/3	First Conference with mainland China on Dementia (in Chinese)	Foundation of Compassion
13/3–15/3	Monastic Experience Camp in English	Humanistic Buddhism Research Centre
14/3	New Year Meeting of FGS volunteers	Dujian Yuan (Supervisor Yuan)
20/3	Devotees' Meeting	Dujian Yuan (Supervisor Yuan)
21/3–22/3	Training for bodhisattva volunteers	FGS volunteers
22/3	Great Compassion Repentance Ritual	Devotee Supervising Office
23/3–29/3	Seven-day Chan Retreat	Pure Chan centre
26/3	International tour of Taiwan (by bicycle)	Buddha Memorial Centre
28/3–29/3	Two days copying sutras	Sutra copying Hall
30/3–31/3	Lecture to FGS mobile library on auditing	FGS Cultural Foundation
Every Sunday	Cultivation on Meritorious family	Home of Merit
Every Sunday	Pilgrimage to the HQ (starts 5:30 a.m.)	Devotee Supervising Office
Chinese New Year Events (Five days)	22:00 Nondurable Gate Open 5:30 Nondurable Gate Open	Devotee Supervising Office

Chapter 7

RITUAL AS SYMPHONY

Ritual, the transfer of merit and honouring the dead

If one surveys the history of Buddhism worldwide, the range of its attitudes to ritual is astonishing. The Buddha held ritual in very low esteem; for him, everything truly important in life took place in the mind. Even in ethics, intention was of paramount importance. He declared *Sīlabbataparāmāso* to be one of the first three fetters[1] that tie us to the cycle of rebirth: it is 'dependence on moral rules and religious vows', an unhealthy attachment. Using the term *sīla*, commonly translated 'morality', with such a negative connotation may at first sight appear puzzling, but in this context it is an aspect of the Buddha's warning against literalism: depending on *sīla* here means regarding morality as a matter of keeping to rules, not of taking responsibility and acting with the best intentions. The only rituals which the Buddha evidently regarded with tolerance were those concerning the dead;[2] of that, more below.

The Emperor Asoka was outspoken in deprecating rituals. In his ninth major rock edict he says that people perform all sorts of rituals for good luck: when someone is ill, for weddings of sons and daughters, for travels, etc.; women in particular perform all kinds of rites which are futile and even disgusting. What really brings good fortune is proper treatment of slaves and servants, respecting one's teachers, self-control in dealing with animals, generosity towards brahmins and

---

1 There are ten such fetters listed, but the first three often appear in texts by themselves; the other two of those three are belief that there is such a thing as permanent existence, and constant uncertainty or dithering.
2 See Richard Gombrich, 'Ambiguity and ambivalence in Buddhist treatment of the dead', *Buddhist Studies Review* 35.1–2 (2018): 97–110.

renouncers, and so forth, and males should inculcate such behaviour in their women.

In the Theravāda tradition, the few rituals laid down for the Saṅgha concern their monastic affairs. The laity are permitted to engage in their own rituals, provided that they do not involve un-Buddhist acts such as blood sacrifice, but in the spirit of Asoka they are regarded by the Saṅgha as useless, a waste of time and money.

By contrast, Chinese culture ever since Confucius has attached great importance to a whole range of rituals, which are felt to dignify and validate life in the family and in society. This has had a profound effect on the practice of Buddhism, and nowhere more than in their treatment of the dead. The cornerstone of Tai Xu's thought when he founded 'Buddhism for Human Life' was his disapproval of the Saṅgha's deep involvement in caring for the dead,[3] particularly one's ancestors; it was by officiating in the cult of ancestors that monastics and their monasteries derived most of their income.

Collectivism as against individual agency in ritual performance

Before we expand on this theme and explore how Hsing Yun has reacted to it, let us draw attention to a dimension of Buddhist practice to which this varying attitude towards ritual is closely connected: the dichotomy between individualism and collective action.

In the religions indigenous to India, there is virtually no such thing as a congregation. When crowds of people converge on a Hindu temple, queue up to make offerings to the deity, maybe offer a prayer and receive blessings, each person is acting on their own behalf and the number of people present has no relevance. Similarly, meditation is an individual, not a collective, activity. A Buddhist will learn meditation from a teacher, but once a pupil has attained a certain level, they go off to somewhere quiet to practise by themselves. While almost any form of religious instruction may be given to more than one pupil at once, the pupils act as individuals just as Hindus do when they visit a temple. In a Theravāda Buddhist monastery there is no such thing as a meditation hall, because there would be no use for it. If several people are jointly involved in a crime or a good deed, they do not acquire 'collective

---

3 Chandler, *Establishing a Pure Land on Earth*, p. 43.

karma', whether bad or good (see Chapter 3: Appendix): the karma attaches to each individual involved according to their motivation.

Since all karma is the responsibility of the individual, no one can save someone else. Even the Buddha cannot. He is infinitely compassionate, but he exercises his compassion by teaching and setting an example; even the most devout follower is solely responsible for their own destiny.

This contrasting view of individual responsibility on the one hand and collective action on the other is a fundamental difference between the Indian and the Chinese assumptions about human life, and it imbues the practice of Indian and Chinese Buddhism respectively. There is however one feature, a feature which, we have seen, probably goes back to the Buddha himself, which the two forms of Buddhism share in their view of responsibility: the transference of merit. How this practice arose has been described at length in Chapter 3 above, but to ensure clarity we repeat the salient points here.

The transfer of merit is a doctrine which came to permeate the whole of Buddhist practice in every Buddhist tradition. It is based on the Buddha's dictum that the moral quality of an act resides solely in the intention behind it. A good intention may evoke a similar good intention in an onlooker, and the latter thereby earns as much merit as the first intender. Thus, if I intend to give a poor man a dollar, someone who learns of my intention may come to feel equally generous and thus develop an intention just like mine – regardless of whether the intention is finally carried out.

The result recalls the English expression of 'having your cake and eating it'. If I want to feed my parents, whether they be alive or dead, that good intention contributes to my store of merit. If someone then learns of my feelings and is inspired to imitate them, they acquire merit too – and this takes away none of my merit.

The practical consequence is that when I do something good, or even just intend to do it, I should inform others about my feelings, because that will inspire them to earn merit for themselves. To hide one's light under a bushel is thus worse than pointless. The English term 'transfer of merit' is however seriously misleading, because nothing gets transferred; but it is like lighting one candle from another. One must remember that in Brahminism/Hinduism one can expunge bad karma from one's record by performing a penance, but this is not so in Buddhism: to avoid paying for bad karma, one can only acquire enough good karma to outweigh it, and mortuary rites give the dead an opportunity for creating good karma by witnessing generous acts and emulating the intentions behind them.

When this topic of merit transfer is mentioned, it is very easy to be misled by the metaphor as if merit were like money, something one can accumulate in a bank account – and many Buddhists do appear to think of it like that.

Historically, the 'transference of merit' entered Buddhism as a concession to the overwhelming desire of Buddhists to 'make merit' which they could pass on to their dead parents, who could no longer act for themselves. This solution was possible because of the Buddha's insistence that merit (or its opposite) could arise only from an individual's desire to do good (or harm) to other people: such a desire is a state of mind, and can be acquired by creatures, regardless of whether they are alive or dead. It is possible because the dead survive as ghosts[4] and can be aware of what their descendants are doing and thinking.

It is hardly an exaggeration to say that the Mahāyāna was constructed by generalizing the transfer of merit and abolishing the condition that it is possible only when the person who receives the merit is aware that it is being transferred to them. A Theravādin who is doing something in thought, word or deed to acquire merit invites (usually by saying so, though a clear thought will suffice) a recipient to 'share' in it as just described; the recipient may be a god (for whom it is easy to be present), a human witness, or the ghost of an ancestor. A Mahāyānist states (or thinks) that all living creatures are welcome to share the merit. No one is bothered by the fact that this noble sentiment contradicts the logic of the original doctrine, because how can everyone be aware of the transfer? On the other hand, in the tradition of Chinese Buddhism, as followed by FGS, the commonest form of communal ritual centres on transferring merit to the dead, particularly to one's own parents and other ancestors. The most important such ritual, held annually by most temples and twice annually in the FGS HQ, is in English called the Water and Land ritual, the Great Compassion, and also referred to as Feeding the Hungry Ghosts.[5]

There is another way in which the Mahāyāna is founded on the idea that merit is transferable. Supremely pure and virtuous beings, whether Buddhas or bodhisattvas, can transfer merit to their worshippers

---

4   We are aware that this is a serious over-simplification – rebirth makes it much more complicated – but it is one that does not affect our argument.

5   See above, Chapter 6 n. 5, for more detail.

and suppliants, and by this act save them from any kind of peril or calamity. They can also save them spiritually. They thus act like gods in some other religions, and their intervention is what Christians call divine grace. They can thus become saviours – as the Buddha of early Buddhism/Theravāda can not.

If one asks why the Buddha of Theravāda does not save people by transferring some of his merit to them, the historian has to reply that the doctrine that the transfer of merit was possible had not yet evolved, and this in turn proves that, as we have explained in Chapter 3 above, the idea of transferring merit appeared first in the context of mortuary rites and ancestor worship, and spread from there. Thus we see that transferring merit to the dead goes back to the very origins of Buddhism, has remained integral to it, and is likely so to continue.

The place of ritual in modern Chinese Buddhism

Holmes Welch wrote *The Practice of Chinese Buddhism 1900-1950* for a wide public, including those who did not know Chinese. Both the vastness of his topic and the nature of his research, which consisted largely of interviewing elderly monks who had fled abroad when the Communists conquered mainland China, set limits to how much he could offer by way of statistical detail and similar minutiae. One must therefore be grateful to Douglas Gildow for his long article 'The Chinese Buddhist ritual field: Common public rituals in PRC monasteries today'.[6] Gildow's article is far from an easy read, because so much of the information is distributed over more than a hundred footnotes, but his passages in continuous prose, particularly the section 'Summary and discussion of the broader relevance of Buddhist ritual life to monasticism' (pp. 84ff.), are more accessible and some are well worth quoting.

> Despite strong criticism from Buddhist reformers over the past century and cycles of state-sponsored suppression under the Communist Party, especially from 1949 until the late 1970s, the performance of rituals is today a central activity for the Saṅgha throughout China. This has not always been the case in the PRC. ... A preface to Mingshan's diary ... claims that the period from 1978 to 1992 involved the 'revival of Buddhist rituals'.

---

6 Douglas Gildow, 'The Chinese Buddhist ritual field: Common public rituals in PRC monasteries today', *Journal of Chinese Buddhist Studies* 27 (2014): 59–127.

100 *Chinese Buddhism Today*

> [P]erforming rituals is today probably the largest single source of revenue for Chinese monastics, as it appears to have been during the Republican period (1912–1949). ... One recent source reported that 40% of the income [of Yufo Monastery in Shanghai] was derived from 'religious ritual and ceremonial services'. Despite its being a major tourist site in Shanghai, income from entrance tickets was only the second largest (28%) source of income.
>
> [T]he performance of rituals continues to exist in tension with other Buddhist practices favored by reformers, such as study and meditation. It is not that *Buddhist* rituals per se are considered ineffective or superstitious. Very few monastics, even radical reformers, have claimed that rituals, properly performed with the right intentions, should never be performed or simply do not work. Rather, common critiques are that rituals are too frequent, taking away time from more valuable activities; too focused on the dead; and too profitable, corrupting monastic into mercenary performers.[7]

Gildow goes on to flesh out these statements with vivid examples. He also reports that Chandler's research implied that for FGS 'donations were most important, ... sale of ritual goods and services was secondary' (Chandler, p. 226). 'In fact, Taiwanese monasteries have major incentives to frame what are in effect sales of goods and services at fixed prices (the prices for which are not written down) as gifts in exchange for donation, because this allows them to avoid paying taxes on the revenue from such transactions'.[8]

The place of ritual in Hsing Yun's world view

Hsing Yun's broadminded versatility enables him to get the best of both worlds, blending pragmatism with piety and compassion. When people say to him, 'You are so busy, you have no time for practice', he replies, 'Practice is serving all sentient beings, fulfilling people's needs and relieving them from suffering. The practice of Buddhism consists of being busy. If you want to be alone, not interacting with people, stay in a coffin'.[9]

An FGS temple is a busy place. The material presented in this book suffices to show that rituals are frequent, but many other activities, all

---

7 The above three paragraphs are taken from Gildow, 'The Chinese Buddhist ritual field', pp. 85–87.
8 Ibid., p. 84, n. 36.
9 Fu, *Chuan Din*, p. 222.

somehow linked to Buddhism, are no less frequent and emphasized. All of these activities are classed as 'communal cultivation' (*gong xiu*); the meaning of this is not clear in English, so we choose to call it simply 'practice', but it should be noted that it is communal, that is, rarely carried out alone. Even a simple thing like meditating on one's breath is usually done along with others.

All practice earns merit, and merit must always be 'transferred'; though this term is widely used, we have shown in Chapter 3, and also above in this chapter, that it might be clearer to say 'shared', but that this is sharing not in the sense of giving some of it away, but in the sense, now common in American English, of giving others access to it. There is a wide range of opinion on whom one shares it with. There are common formulae for sharing it with all sentient beings. In chapter VII, 'Rites for the dead',[10] of his great book, Welch goes into far more detail on these matters than we can reproduce here. In formal contexts it is more common to share it with the dead in general[11]; and this in turn may be confined specifically to dead members of one's family. Similarly, sharing with the living may be confined to one's own relatives. How one is sharing is often determined only by the intentions of the sharer, so that an observer cannot be sure what is going on in people's minds.

Welch writes: 'It would have been unfilial to suppose that [one's] father had deserved to be reborn as a hungry ghost, but it would have been even more unfilial to neglect the appropriate measures if he were one'.[12] If one transfers merit to one's own dead parents there is a feeling that this implies that they are living as hungry ghosts, and people may try to avoid that implication by generalizing the transfer; but the underlying spirit of what goes on is certainly focused on one's dead ancestors. FGS teaches that when one makes and transfers merit, a fixed proportion of it goes to the dead and the rest to its donor, but there is no agreement what the figures are,[13] and we have explained why this is bound to be so (see Chapter 3).

Not all rituals require that members of the Saṅgha officiate, but the more important ones do, and monasteries in traditional Chinese Buddhism were involved with the cult of ancestors to a degree which

---

10 Welch, *The Practice of Chinese Buddhism*, pp. 179–205.
11 Ibid., p. 183.
12 Ibid., pp. 183–84.
13 In a previous article, 'Christianity as model and analogue', p. 230, we have given a precise figure, told to us by an informant; we did not then realize that the figure varies.

scandalized Tai Xu. As custodians of the tablets which represented dead individuals and as officiants at funerary and commemorative rites, the Saṅgha were paid fees for their services, and these were usually their main source of income.[14] Hsing Yun has greatly diminished the importance of this aspect of religious practice, but he has by no means abolished it. His evaluation of rituals was ambivalent: he said much in favour of the rituals and even of their importance, but if he had criticized them too strongly he would not only have scandalized the people, he would also have deprived his movement of a source of income which remained important even after he had introduced a vast range of other ways for the movement to make money.[15] His frequent lowering of fees for the Saṅgha's ritual performances also worked to increase the number of laity who could afford to be involved.

The main activities in the rituals practised by the FGS are purification (by sprinkling water); chanting texts (mostly in classical Chinese); and worship of Buddhas and bodhisattvas, both in general and specifically, by offering them lamps, incense, flowers and food. For major rituals participants must pay a fixed financial contribution (which Hsing Yun tries to keep at a modest level). Quite a few rituals involve repentance (*chan* or *chanhui*): the repentance consists in chanting the appropriate texts, and the good karma from the chanting is thought to cancel the bad karma one has previously incurred. Bottles of water may be left in front of a Buddha image during chanting; the water thus empowered is taken away for healing and other benign purposes. Traditionally captive animals are released at some point in the ceremony, but Hsing Yun does not favour this ritual so FGS tends not to practise it.

As explained in Chapter 6 above, the largest rite has several different names, including the Japanese name *obon*. Most temples carry it out once a year, the traditional date being 15 July by the lunar calendar. It lasts several days and tends to be expensive for the leading participants. The FGS became famous for its performance of this rite and now gives it twice a year at the HQ, besides often co-operating with performances at branch temples. A performance includes all the lesser rites in the liturgical calendar except such things as birthdays.

---

14 'Taixu gave this as a fundamental reason for the lack of interest in Buddhist teachings among the young and intellectuals'. Chandler, *Establishing a Pure Land on Earth*, p. 231.
15 On the mainland, many monasteries were landowners, another good source of income, but in Taiwan hardly any temples own land. For a table showing income sources for mainland temples and FGS, see Ibid., p. 233.

Ritual as symphony   103

When one surveys what Hsing Yun has remarked in regard to this major ritual, one is struck by how little he has to say about the repentance which seems to be at its core, and how much about the music, a theme intimately connected with togetherness. The role he ascribes to music is reminiscent, from a slightly different perspective, of what we have quoted in a previous article from Tai Xu's remarks about Christian church attendance on Sundays: 'they all worship with the same music and rituals, and this uniformity has a profound impact on their families. Thus the harmonic music and solemn rites mould family life and develop organizational ability'.[16]

Hsing Yun says[17] that rituals should be enjoyable and draw people into Buddhism. Rituals help you to realize your own Buddha nature, which you do by your own power, not that of other beings.

The relationship between the ritual of Water and Land, Obon, and the ceremony celebrating Bhaiṣajya Guru ('the Medicine Buddha') and the other rites with which these partly overlap and/or coincide, is complex, and we suspect that only specialists fully understand it. This applies to every aspect: the rites, the words chanted, and the music performed. To anyone interested in the music, we strongly recommend the wonderful publication by Reed Criddle,[18] which we became aware of only as this book was going to press. Prof. Criddle was able to record two entire annual performances at Fo Guang Shan, and to discuss them with participants.

The chanting shares important characteristics with other aspects of the performance. For example, what really counts is not any recording or transcription of a chant but each rendition by an individual, even though each individual is mostly performing as part of an ensemble. No two performances are exactly the same. Slight deviations, whether it be of the music or of the words chanted, are not frowned upon but on the contrary encouraged, while insistence on precise replication is considered a form of attachment, and thus contrary to the spirit of Buddhism.

In the FGS performances, the chanting was divided between eight choruses singing at different shrines; their chants were in several

---

16 Yao and Gombrich, 'Christianity as model and analogue', p. 209.
17 We are relying in this section mainly on HY's writings on the internet at http://www.masterhsingyun.org/: 'A hundred talks on Saṅgha affairs', no. 14, 'Congregation and collective practice'.
18 See Bibliography.

sections, spread over two days, each section lasting about two hours. Somewhat surprisingly, even though the performances had so many irregularities, each section ended almost simultaneously. Each of the eight choirs was headed by an experienced chanter, usually an elderly nun, who sang the first few notes alone, and by that fragment of chant set the pitch for the rest of the two-hour performance. Where the pitch went too low for a chanter, it was normal for a nun to remain silent and for a monk (or other male) to go an octave higher.

A single person chanting is like one lighted match, but communal chanting is a great fire. To practise collectively maximizes the merit. If a person does not understand the content of the practice, it does not matter. It is not absolutely necessary to have full concentration if you are participating in a group; the merit still accrues, because our hearts work together and create the power of a great wave. In this way, everyone gets overwhelmed by the sentiments of the Dharma. Each member also gets the merit of the collective.

People's voices chant at various pitches, so the effect is harmonious, like a great choir. The Saṅgha must lead, and the lay congregation follow. The wooden fish is a great help to inspire chanting; its beat leads, so the beater must not make any mistakes. If the Saṅgha keep together when chanting, that shows they are a good Saṅgha. Hsing Yun prefers that there be a lot of instruments accompanying the chanting. The beater of the wooden fish can be any monastic but at the most solemn moments it is normally a monk.

In general, chanting together and with the heart is the main thing, more important than getting the words right. Everyone is both giver and taker, so the merit is multiplied. A two-hour session of chanting is fine for the Saṅgha, but too long for the laity nowadays. As a child, he would stand chanting for hours on end, but most people prefer to sit and that is OK too. People can prostrate to any Buddha, even to those we do not understand. But after every service we must give a lecture and explain to the congregation the meaning of what we have been doing and the story behind it.

Already in 1963, Hsing Yun displayed considerable ambivalence towards chanting as an occupation for the Saṅgha:

> Among Buddhist monastics, the best will become abbots and abbesses; the weakest will be chanting for ritual (*jian chan*) and seeking donations (*hua yuan*). Other young monks and nuns will spend their precious lives on lengthy chanting morning and evening and cleaning the monasteries. In more than ten years they will only have learnt to

sweep the floor and chant, nothing else. This is a very serious problem for Buddhism.[19]

In his biography of the Buddha, Hsing Yun wrote that the Buddha's disciple Ānanda had a set of dreams which the Buddha interpreted for him. The fifth dream was of a great sandalwood tree with many wild boars digging at its roots and thus threatening to destroy it. The Buddha says that this means that after his death 'monks will not aspire to spread the true teachings. They will only care for their own living conditions. They will sell my image and conduct ceremonies for their livelihoods'.[20]

Whether it is Chan or Pure Land does not matter. In mediaeval times services were arranged on fixed schedules, but nowadays we can be completely flexible and the spontaneity makes things come to life. Repentance services differ greatly in how simple or complicated they are, and thus in their demand on clerical manpower. One must suit the congregation and adapt to the occasion. It is unnecessary to hold rituals in temples; we can also use sites associated with other communities. However, every temple should have not just a lay congregation but an attached member of the Saṅgha to lead it.

Funerals

Funerals are an obvious focal point for any survey of Chinese Buddhist practice. Tai Xu referred to his project for the wholesale reform of Buddhism in China as 'Buddhism for the living'. The funeral rites at which the body was cremated in a coffin, along with Buddhist objects, were elaborate and expensive. The ashes were kept in a jar, labelled with the name of the deceased, in a section of a Buddhist temple, and on the anniversaries of the deceased's birth and death the monastics conducted rituals, again often elaborate and expensive, to earn merit for the dead. Most of the rituals involved chanting by monastics, for which they were paid fees by the descendants, and in many cases a large part of a monastery's income depended on the services performed for the dead. The ideology of filial piety ensured that most descendants

---

19 'Doing What?' ('Zuo shen mo?'), *Awakening*, 21 May 1963.
20 Ven. Master Hsing Yun, *The Biography of Sakyamuni Buddha*, trans. Alex Wong (Los Angeles: Buddha's Light Publishing, 2013), p. 396. Original Chinese ed. 1955–58.

did their duty on a generous scale. Traditional celebration of funerals in this style is by no means obsolete.

Hsing Yun has not attempted to abolish funerary rituals or commemorative rites for the dead. Not only would this have been shocking to the sentiments of his followers: completely to forego this major source of income would have been foolhardy. However, he has given free rein to his spirit of innovation. Naturally, he has written a lot about death and funerals; we shall largely confine ourselves to drawing on a speech he gave at Xi Lai University on 3 March 2006.[21]

He began by mentioning the cycle of rebirth. Tradition has it that birth is happy, death is sad; but death is as inevitable as birth. The associated rituals should be understood as opportunities to benefit the dead. If it seems that someone is bound to die before very long, it is good to build up a relationship with a nearby temple where the funeral can be arranged.

The dying person may be moved to a hospice, where clean air, subdued lighting and Buddhist images create a calm atmosphere. One can then preach to the dying person about the Western Paradise which they are soon to enter, and they may join in the chanting which accompanies the sermon. 'Assisted dying' (*lin zhuong zhu nian*), chanting which may be either by monastics or laity, can also be arranged. However, it is by no means necessary that the chanting before or during funerals be done by monastics, so it need not cost anything. It may even be supplied by a recording rather than by a congregation.

It is not necessary to have long or costly funeral services or to have lots of strangers in attendance. A private service for family and close friends is perfectly satisfactory; when his own mother died (aged 95) HY did not want any stranger to be involved in her funeral service. Alternatively, the funeral can be combined with another service at a temple. Money thus saved can instead be spent on an educational or charitable cause; the merit accruing from this may raise the dead person's status in the next life.

A funeral service should be simple and dignified; it need not consist of more than putting the body in a coffin and cremating it, and a couple of hours is quite long enough. Giving a banquet is counter-productive, because preparing the food involves killing, bad karma which will

---

21 http://www.masterhsingyun.org/: Seminar on Humanist Buddhism and contemporary social issues; section on life and death, vol. 2: 'Buddhist funeral customs'.

negate what we hope to do for the dead person. Acts of merit performed within 49 days of the death will benefit the dead person. On the other hand, there is no room for the various superstitions one sees in Taiwan, such as using geomancy to determine details, finding an auspicious date for the funeral, processions, or public displays of grief and lamentation. Similarly, there is a popular belief that the body should not be moved within eight hours of death; this is pointless, and in any case when exactly death occurs is controversial.

Though chanting is not strictly necessary, it may be helpful to the dead. The dead person is like a stone, weighed down by their bad karma, and they have to pass to the next life, which may be compared to crossing a river. Chanting is then like a boat to carry the stone and ease the transition.

For those who would like guidance on the details of holding a funeral, Hsing Yun has provided three possible orders of service. We here reproduce the most elaborate of the three.[22]

1. Lotus Pond prayer.
2. Chant name of Amitābha x 3.
3. Chant *Amitābha Sūtra*.
4. Mantra of rebirth.
5. Mantra for offering food.
6. Verses praising Amitābha.
7. Chanting Amitābha's name, while putting the corpse into the coffin (*ru lian*).
8. Taking the three Refuges.
9. Transfer of merit.

FGS ritual overseas

We have given the reader a sketch of Hsing Yun's attitude to ritual, and tried to frame it by referring to mainstream Buddhist ritual practice on the mainland and to the attitude of Tai Xu and other reformers to that practice. To complete the picture, let us quote a few words from an extremely recent source: Jen Reinke's article 'Sacred secularities:

---

22 http://www.masterhsingyun.org/: Collection of Buddhism, section 6, death ritual, 3. Funeral (*shan zang dian yi*).

108 *Chinese Buddhism Today*

Ritual and social engagement in a global Buddhist China'.[23] Thus if our material from Chandler, Welch and Gildow may be said to tell us about the past, and our further research about the very recent past, Reinke's is so recent that he may be allowing us to glimpse the future. He does not omit, however, to write, albeit briefly, about Tai Xu's ideal for what a temple should be doing: in a *renjian* temple, 'dharma assemblies are conducted in order to create merits for the victims of [the] natural disasters that occur worldwide'.[24]

Reinke has observed the operations of Fo Guang Shan in the English-speaking world (South Africa and the USA), as well as in Taiwan, China, Hong Kong and Germany. The article from which we are quoting concerns what happens in and around the Xi Lai Temple founded in Los Angeles in 1978:

> There are many rituals at the temple, including large scale ones like the Emperor Liang Repentance Service ... and even, on very special occasions, the biggest and most elaborate of the Chinese Buddhist rituals: the Water Land Liberation Service ... One of the regular rituals, ... conducted monthly, is the Great Compassion Repentance Service ... It is praised for cleansing the minds of the devotees and attendance is normally so high that the main shrine is not big enough to hold all the people, [and the overflow] have to make do with a video transmission ... The ceremony consists of the introduction and the chanting of the Great Compassion Mantra while seated and while circum-ambulating through the shrine room. At the end of the ceremony, the names of all the donors are recited and everyone attending receives a bottle of water that is blessed through the recitation of the mantra.
>
> On its website the Xi Lai Temple states: 'Some of the merits often associated with the Great Compassion Mantra are: rebirth into higher realms, meeting beneficial acquaintances, having competent facilities (*sic*), bountiful food and wealth, gaining great respect, and the opportunity to learn Buddhist teachings. Moreover, those who recite this mantra will not suffer death by starvation, disease, poison, flood, or fire. Water blessed with the great Compassion Mantra is called the Great Compassion Water, and is taken by devotees for its spiritually cleansing qualities'.[25]

---

23 Jen Reinke, 'Sacred secularities: Ritual and social engagement in a global Buddhist China', *Religions* [MDPI journal], 31 October 2018, pp. 1–12.
24 Ibid., p. 6.
25 Ibid. We have omitted the Chinese names of the rites. For details, including how they are related, see Chapter 6, n. 5, above. That material is drawn from different sources. As there is no central authority, some variation in practice

Reinke comments:

> To volunteer at the temple is not just a way to contribute and thereby practice *dāna* [giving], but the most efficient way to practice the Buddhist path as a whole. Other Socially Engaged Buddhists who perceive social involvement within secular society as religious activity in itself, often do so at the expense of more 'traditional' forms of Buddhist religiosity. ... Fo Guang Shan reformulates the 'traditional' practices of Chinese Buddhism (particularly ritual, but also study, meditation, chanting, etc.) in a contemporary, accessible manner. The sacred, that can be experienced through the more traditional practices, is then to be actualized through volunteer work in the secular sphere.[26]

Thus, smoothly recapitulating in a couple of pages the entire journey from Tai Xu, who invented *renjian* Buddhism, to Chinese and Taiwanese immigrants in Los Angeles, who live their Buddhism through what Thich Nhat Hanh deliberately renamed 'engaged Buddhism', Reinke has summarized the whole story, a narrative which takes us from what many Anglophones still call the Far East to the Far West. More importantly, this journey takes us straight from the world in which one's religion has its heart in rituals undertaken communally in sanctified premises along with other people of the same cultural background, to where it has become what is essentially practised by individuals, acting wherever they are in the wider world, however, and among whomever they see fit, creating what they hold sacred as they go along. In the fewest words: Protestantism has totally reshaped Buddhism.

---

and nomenclature is to be expected. Note how the benefits listed combine those with an archaic and those with a more modern flavour.

26 Ibid., p. 7.

Chapter 8

FO GUANG SHAN'S ACTIVITIES: EDIFICATION THROUGH SPECTACLE AND ENTERTAINMENT

In 1998 Master Hsing Yun was entrusted with the custody of a relic, one of the Buddha's teeth; the ceremony took place in Bangkok at the HQ of the World Fellowship of Buddhists, of which Hsing Yun remains Hon. President. In order to house this in sufficient sanctity and splendour, he had built at FGS the Buddha Memorial Center (BMC).[1] This is not a single building but a huge complex that exhibits to the public what Hsing Yun, who designed it, considers the essentials of Buddhism. This complex was opened to the public late in 2011, and at the time of writing (2017–18), has recently been completed by erecting in the middle a new College of Humanistic Buddhism.

It also features a Historical Museum. The museum produces an illustrated folding leaflet, from which we learn that FGS has 'the objectives of propagating Buddhism through culture, fostering talent through education, benefiting society through charity, and purifying the human mind through cultivation to advance Buddhism past the new milestone of modernization and spread Humanistic Buddhism from Taiwan to the world'. The aim of Buddhism is thus not to help people to escape from life, but to show them how to solve its problems by deploying their talents. They should engage with society, not avoid it, and eliminate obsolete customs and prejudices.

In this same pamphlet we read of Hsing Yun: 'His arhat shoes leave behind traces of four-colored lotus flowers, and his waving robe sleeves produce Pure Lands with seven gems'. In the very next paragraph we read: 'Throughout his life, the Venerable Master Hsing Yun never

---

1 We also use this abbreviation, italicized, to refer to the book about BMC of which full details are given below.

received a formal education and never received an official diploma. ... His every thought, spoken word, and action all abide by the principle of being an ordinary monk who never does anything that is not for Buddhism'.

This well illustrates the double vision presented to devotees throughout the FGS: the Master is at the same time an enlightened being (the charismatic side) and an ordinary monk without even the advantages of a superior education (the pragmatic side). Similarly, FGS pragmatically sets about turning our world into a Pure Land (a heaven on earth, a Christian would say), but in fact that Pure Land is already here, constantly evoked in art, music, rituals, and the never-failing benignity of the Master.

Figure 8: Carnival of All Deities held at the HQ, Gaoxiong, 25 December 2018

Buddha Land in the Human World: The Making of the Buddha Memorial Center (BMC)

Written by Pan Xuan with Venerable Master Hsing Yun

First English edition 2013, Buddha's Light Publishing, Hacienda Heights, CA, USA; trans. Robert Smitheram

Ed. Fo Guang Shan International Translation Center, pp. xvii, 340.

The following inscription by Master Hsing Yun, in Chinese and English,[2] is on the wall of the entrance of the Buddha Memorial Center.

> In February 1998, as I realised that the Bhikkhuni Precepts[3] have been lost in the Theravāda tradition, I held a Bodh Gaya international Full Ordination in India, in order to restore the Chinese Buddhist history, crossing the boundaries of nations' and races' Dharma lineage. Not only did this see to the restoration of the vinaya[4] within the Theravāda Bhikkhuni Saṅgha; another extraordinary event was also accomplished. That is, Tibetan Lama Kunga Dorje Rinpoche intended to give me the Buddha's tooth relic, which had been under his safekeeping for many years, hoping that I would bring it back to Taiwan and build a memorial center to enshrine it, so as to ensure the everlasting Buddha's light to shine and the revival of the relic's glory ... According to the Buddha's sutras, after the Buddha entered parinirvana,[5] he left behind three tooth relics in the human world. Currently, one is located in Sri Lanka, one is in mainland China, and the third was originally kept in India but during the Muslim invasion was secretly taken from the great Buddhist college of Nalanda to Tibet and enshrined in the Sakya Namgyal monastery. In 1968 that temple was destroyed in the cultural revolution and the whereabouts of this third tooth relic became unknown.
>
> As it turned out, the relic had been found by Tibetan Lama Kunga Dorje Rinpoche. In order to guard it, he risked his life by crossing the Himalayas and travelled a long and arduous journey to India. After authentication by his own Master and several elder masters, the tooth relic was stored for 30 years in his own secret box.
>
> In 1998, when I went to India to transmit the Full Ordination Precepts, Kunga Dorje Rinpoche realized that he was already very old and had slim hope of returning to Tibet. Furthermore, he was unable to build a temple to enshrine the relic in India, so he decided to find someone to whom the relic could be entrusted. He learned that Fo Guang Shan established the Chinese Han-Tibet Culture Association to enhance Han and Tibetan cultural exchange, and even held a World Tantric and Sutric Buddhist Conference despite all practical difficulties. At the same time, Fo Guang also organized the World Fellowship of Buddhists conference and established the Buddha's Light International Association (BLIA). Being very touched by Fo Guang Shan's endeavor in promoting world Buddhist exchange, and knowing that it is a legitimate Buddhist order that promotes

---

2 We have slightly edited the first part of the English text, using *BMC*, p. 30. The footnotes are added by us.
3 The rules for fully ordained nuns.
4 Monastic Rule.
5 The death of the Buddha's body.

Humanistic Buddhism with branch temples throughout the world, he believed that I would have the ability to guard and preserve the Buddha's tooth relic. Thus through the help of Lama Tien Bi-Shuang, he personally expressed his wish to give the tooth relic to me during my visit to India for the precept transmission.

What happened next is recorded in BMC (pp. 32–36). Kunga Dorje Rinpoche left India on 6 April 1998, travelling to Thailand via Nepal. He carried the relic on his person. At the Fo Guang Shan Centre in Bangkok it was enshrined in the Buddha Hall. On April 8, the Buddha's birthday in the Chinese Buddhist calendar, the Rinpoche personally gave it to Lama Tien Pi-Shuang and it was taken to the premises of the World Fellowship of Buddhists, where it was formally handed over to Master Hsing Yun. The next day the relic was flown to Taiwan.

As a motorcade brought the relic from the airport to Songshang railway station, 'a miracle occurred'. The Ven Tzu Jung[6] remembered that it was raining heavily, but 'as soon as I stepped out of the car, I still felt a couple of drops of rain, but then, in an instant, it stopped! It seemed as if the downpour had been cut off with a knife, the rain stopped smooth and clean'. It was 'as if heaven had sent the rain specifically to purify the sanctuary' which had been erected on Songlong Road, outside the station. Then, 'as it was getting dark, a beam of light shot out of the sky and flooded Songlong Road with a golden light'. This was visible on the TV transmissions of the scene. One of the commentators, the Ven Yi Fa, exclaimed, 'This is the Buddha's light that shines everywhere, and so this is the path of the Buddha's light!'

For eight months, the relic was enshrined in Fo Guang Shan's Taipei Vihara.[7] 'On December 12th, the reliquary containing the Buddha's tooth relic boarded a train especially reserved for it by the Taiwan Railway Administration for its journey south', and after travelling by an indirect route it reached FGS the next day.

The Buddhist Memorial Center, covering a hundred hectares, was opened to the public in 2011. The day of the opening was arranged to coincide with the centenary of the founding of the Republic of China, 25 December.[8]

The Center lies next to the monastery, about 17 kilometres from the city of Gaoxiong. Before the Center opened, this area was not easy to

---

6   Tzu Jung and Yi Fa (below) are Buddhist nuns attached to FGS.
7   The branch monastery in the capital.
8   The coincidence with Christmas Day is not relevant.

reach except by car, but since the opening a fast bus runs every half hour to and from the main line railway station in Gaoxiong, a journey of nearly 40 minutes.

Entry is free, and so are refreshments within the Center, though one is encouraged to make a donation (and surely most people do so).

The Center officially has the capacity to hold some 25,000 visitors at a time, but these figures are easily exceeded on public holidays. Indeed, it is estimated that in 2012 on the first three days of the Chinese New Year, there were more than two hundred thousand visitors.

The entire content and layout of the Center are planned by the Master himself. They are designed to edify the public and educate them in Buddhism, but the details of the architecture, iconography, etc. do not follow tradition closely; information is largely conveyed by captions. For example, as one advances from the main entrance, whether one walks down the left aisle or the right, one passes a long series of murals which illustrate in vivid and even gruesome detail the horrors faced by members of the animal kingdom due to human failure to live on a vegetarian diet. We even see tethered domestic animals shedding large tears at the approach of the butcher. These are enlarged copies (many of them, it must be confessed, rather crude) of a series of 86 paintings which the Chinese mainland artist Feng Zikai (1898–1975) created over 46 years.

While the Center's overall artistic aim is to evoke the India of the Buddha's day, the style of the buildings is eclectic, freely combining Indian and Chinese elements, and there are many features designed chiefly to make the whole more attractive to the unsophisticated, e.g. life-size free-standing statues of elephants.

The style of the tourist facilities is modern: for example, in the entrance hall there are a Starbucks coffee shop, a restaurant, a bank, a post office, as well as the inevitable gift shop and stalls selling Buddhist souvenirs.

The scale of everything is immense. For example, fifty mature Bodhi and banyan trees were transplanted to here from a public elementary school in the area. We are told that all the trees were donated, and their survival rate after being replanted was ninety-nine per cent (*BMC*, p. 197).

Chapter 9

OFFSHOOTS OF FGS

In traditional Buddhism, schism is very carefully defined. It is an event which takes place within the Saṅgha and has no formal effect on the laity – and this remains true of the FGS. There is no official record of when a monk or nun leaves the FGS. In some years more have left than have been ordained, but it is impossible to find out how many have left, let alone their names. We had thought of ending this book with a chapter on schismatics, but soon realized that this is not possible. The best we can do is to supply three cases in which we know that men ordained in FGS have gone off to start institutions of their own. Though they are all men, we know that they have some female disciples. We call their movements 'offshoots'.

Ling Jiu Mountain monastery[1]

Ven. Xin Dao (alternative spelling: Hsintao) was born in 1948 in Lashio, Myanmar, with the name of Yang Xiaosheng. He founded the Ling Jiu Mountain Buddhist Foundation in Taiwan in 1989. Xin Dao is well known for his work on interfaith dialogue, especially on dialogue with Muslims.

Xin Dao's family had emigrated to Myanmar from Yunnan, southeast China. At the age of nine, he joined a guerrilla group and engaged in warfare against the communists for the next four years. Then, when he was 13 years old, he followed the Republic of China Army to Taiwan. While he was serving in the army he became interested in Yiguangdao, a religion of vegetarianism, and became a vegetarian at the age of 15. He was discharged at the age of 20.

---

1 Information mostly from https://www.hsintao.org, but some data seem to be garbled.

In 1973, aged 25, he was ordained as a novice by Hsing Yun and joined the FGS Saṅgha. He entered the FGS seminary, but did not stay at FGS very long. In the next year, he moved to a mountain area of Taipei, Waishuangsi, where he began to meditate for 18 hours a day. In 1975 he went on retreat in a remote cemetery in Longtan in Yilan county, where he increased his meditation to 20 hours per day. In 1982 he began a six-month retreat, with long fasts in which he took neither food nor water. In 1983 he moved to the Fulong mountain area, where his daily diet was nine Chinese herb pills and spring water. That year he founded the Ling Jiu Mountain monastery (Gṛdhrakūṭa in Sanskrit). Through the success of the monastery, in 2001 Xin Dao founded the Museum of World Religions in New Taipei city; it was the first museum of this type in Taiwan. In 2002 he also founded the Global Family for Love and Peace in New York, USA. Being interested in interfaith dialogue, Xin Dao also serves on the Board of World Religious Leaders for the Elijah Interfaith Institute.[2]

Xin Dao claims that he has received three Buddhist traditions. Firstly, the Chinese Mahāyāna tradition. He was tonsured by Master Hsing Yun, and also received the Dharma Seal from Ven. Master Benhuan to become the 44th successor of Linji School; in 2013 he was appointed by Hsing Yun to be the 49th holder of the FGS Linji School.

Secondly, Xin Dao has also received the Theravāda tradition. In 1994 he went to Myanmar to receive Arhat precepts[3] by attending a Theravāda Three Ordination Platforms[4] Transmission; then he toured Myanmar and visited various Buddhist monasteries and enlightened masters. He was honoured with the title of National Master by the Burmese government. Since then, Xin Dao has dressed in Theravāda style.

In 2001, Xin Dao was given the name Pelgi Dorje (Auspicious Vajra) by the Katok Moktsa Rinpoche of Nyingma Katok Lineage. In May Xin Dao travelled to Xikang, China to receive blessings. In 2002, Bairo Rinpoche delegated Moktsa Rinpoche to perform a ceremony for Xin Dao in recognition of the value of his transmission.

---

2 This is a UNESCO-sponsored interfaith organization founded in Jerusalem in 1997 by Rabbi Alon Goshen-Gottstein.
3 We know of nothing in the Theravāda tradition that is called 'Arhat precepts', but assume that it alludes to one of the sets of precepts found in Theravāda.
4 Like the topic of the previous note, we take this to be a misunderstanding by a Chinese translator. The Three Ordination Platforms is an important ritual in Chinese Buddhism but unknown to Theravāda.

Apart from introducing various secular subjects into Buddhism, Xin Dao also expands the traditional Water and Land service onto a larger scale, which he calls the Water, Land and Sky Service; this enables him to draw a larger range of participants to the ceremony.

Nanhai Buddhist Association (*nanhai jiangtan*)[5]

The Nanhai Buddhist Association was founded by Ven. Huiye (1950s–) in the 1990s. Huiye was born on Green Island (Ludao, a fishing island near the Philippines), Taiwan, into a fishing family. Soon the family moved to the main island, Taidon, for education. Since the family was very poor, Huiye only managed to have an elementary education; then he began to learn to be a carpenter. The family survived through repeated help from Buddhists. Subsequently Huiye was told that he could become a novice of FGS, where he could have plenty of food and shelter. Thus he joined the Saṅgha in his teens.

For more than three decades Huiye was working like a donkey. Because he did not enjoy studying, he did not go to the FGS seminary; instead he used most of his craft skills for decorating venues of ceremonies. He was very good at chanting in a loud voice.

One day in the 1990s, when he was in his forties, he could no longer stand the bullying of a senior FGS nun, so he left and founded the Nanhai Buddhist centres by himself; he now has five centres in Taiwan.

He now has 70 to 80 Saṅgha, of both genders, working with him, all ex-FGS. He concentrates on organizing Water and Land rituals, and he plans to found a temple for this purpose in Malaysia. He also hopes to found an orphanage in Cambodia where he can train the children to become Buddhist monastics.

Amitofo Care Centre (ACC)[6]

The ACC was founded by Ven. Hui Li (b.1955) in 2001, firstly in Malawi, then with three further centres elsewhere in Africa.

Ven. Hui Li was born into a poor family in Pindong, southern Taiwan. He used to work as a night security guard when he was in middle school to pay his tuition fees. While he studied in high school he had to live

---

5 All info from a personal interview with Ven. Hui Ye.
6 Info from web page: baike.baidu.com.

at a temple for free; there he began to learn Buddhism. The Sutra of the Sixth Patriarch was his introduction to Buddhism, and he became a vegetarian.

In 1974 he was tonsured by Hsing Yun and received full ordination precepts. He graduated from the FGS graduate seminary, then became the chairperson for the FGS general office, superintendent of the male Saṅgha, and construction supervisor of the FGS Executive Council.

In 1992, he responded to Hsing Yun's proposal to found an FGS temple in South Africa. In ten years he had founded and become the abbot of the biggest Mahāyāna temple, the Nanhua temple in Johannesburg. After seeing the poverty and weakness of Buddhism in Africa, Hui Li vowed to die in Africa and to serve the African Blacks with five reincarnations. He survived a traffic accident which was almost fatal, and many bouts of malaria, and claimed that those experiences would make him a real 'African'.

In 2001 Hui Li left the Nanhua temple and travelled deeper into Africa to spread the seed of Buddhism. He visited Malawi, Tanzania, Zimbabwe, Chad, Nigeria, Cameroun, Ghana, Burkina Faso, Congo, Senegal, Libya, Swaziland and Lesotho. He recruited students for his Buddhist seminary, took care of orphans and conducted compassionate relief. In 1994 he founded the first Buddhist seminary in Africa. Since then he has engaged ten African Buddhist nuns, some of whom began to preach in Africa while some stayed in FGS HQ. (The latter have even learnt Hokkien.)

Amitofo Care Centre (ACC) was founded by Hui Li in 2005 in Malawi, with the aim of serving 2,000 orphans. The centre will establish an AIDs care centre, a vocational centre and a Buddhist seminary. Hui Li believes that Africa will provide the future human resources for the Buddhist Saṅgha, which is why he wants to place an orphanage there.

Africa is the desert of Buddhism, but due to his strength and diligence, Hui Li's African project is supported by his foundations back in Taiwan: the Yuanjui Educational Fund and the Puxian Humanitarian Association are non-profit organizations dedicated to backing Hui Li's mission in Africa. The great vow of Hui Li has won him the title of 'the African monk'.

Update: article by Ven. Ben Xing

As we were finishing this book, we came across an article on the internet[7] which enables us to carry the story slightly further. The article on the website 'Buddhistdoor Global' is dated 29 December 2016 and titled 'Nurturing the roots of Chinese Buddhism in Africa'.

The author, Ben Xing, writes largely in the first person, and the rest of this chapter contains an excerpt from his article (which is about double this length).

He begins:

> I was born Simon Manase Masauko in Malawi on 23 April 1978. I received the Dharma name Ben Xing, which means 'awakening' or, more literally, 'the original root of awakening', in 2000 from the renowned Buddhist monk Venerable Master Hui Li, the first Mahāyāna monk from Taiwan to come to Africa and propagate Humanistic Buddhism.

> Ven. Master Hui Li, who had a vision of planting the seeds of the Buddhadharma among Africa's youth, is one of the founding members of the African Buddhist College, which has since trained more than 500 monastics from the Congo Madagascar, Malawi, Mozambique, Tanzania, South Africa, and Zimbabwe. He is also the founder of Amitofo Care Centres in Africa and across the world … In 1999, I became one of six people from Malawi to undertake a three-year monastic training course at the African Buddhist College in South Africa … We studied and practiced Humanistic Buddhism, which derives from Mahāyāna Buddhism…

> I later encountered the same practices when I furthered my studies in 2002 at Tsung-Lin Male University in Taiwan under the Fo Guang Shan monastic order. We were asked to abide by the Five Precepts that all Buddhists live by, refraining from: harming living things, taking what is not given, sexual misconduct, lying and gossiping, and consuming intoxicating substances … In 2003, I furthered my studies in Myanmar, practicing Theravāda Buddhism at the International Theravada Buddhist Missionary University, where the teachings focused on self-salvation, vigorous meditation, and becoming an *arhat*…

> If Buddhism could adopt some of the ways and methodologies that the Catholic Church has applied in Malawi, I have no doubt that many people would embrace the religion and its profound teachings. In my view, the Catholic system of practice has similarities to Buddhism in that both have male and female monastic communities that practice

---

7 https://www.buddhistdoor.net/features/
nurturing-the-roots-of-chinese-buddhism-in-africa

celibacy and abide by a monastic code of conduct. Catholicism has prevailed and prospered in Africa because it has accepted African traditions and empowered a certain group of locals as representatives, while their missionaries have adopted local customs, eat local food, and speak the local languages. The Catholic Church has benefited and still benefits the locals at a national level, while I view Buddhism as conservative in its presentation and I think it will be some decades before it embraces Africans as family members.

He concludes:

In a nutshell, I am truly grateful to Venerable Hui Li and to everyone who has contributed positively to the propagation of Buddhism in Africa as it has not only given me an opportunity to study and practice the profound teachings of the Buddha, but has also enabled many students from across Africa to study the Dharma. Buddhism still needs more support in terms of local pioneers who understand the teachings and its concepts on a deeper level and who can pass them on to others. We need resources such as English-language books on Buddhism, which can be distributed to all national and private libraries, primary and secondary schools, and universities. We also need to form local Buddhist associations that can present Buddhist ideas by calling on graduates of the African Buddhist College to be the torchbearers of the Buddhadharma.

Figure 9: The article includes a group photo: 'Master Hsing Yun and Master Hui Li with African Buddhist disciples'. Hsing Yun is seated in the front row, 4th from the spectator's right, wearing a rosary. The tall monk seated to his left is presumably Ven. Hui Li.

BIBLIOGRAPHY

Chandler, Stuart. *Establishing a Pure Land on Earth: The Foguang Buddhist Perspective on Modernization and Globalization*. Honolulu: University of Hawai'i Press, 2004.

Chiu, Tzu-lung. 'Rethinking the precept of not taking money in contemporary Taiwanese and mainland Chinese Buddhist nunneries'. *Journal of Buddhist Ethics* 21 (2014): 1–56.

Cho, Francisca. 'Buddhism and science: Translating and re-translating culture', in David L. McMahan (ed.), *Buddhism in the Modern World*. Abingdon and New York: Routledge, 2012: 273–88.

Criddle, Reed (ed.). *Chanting the Medicine Buddha Sutra: A Musical Transcription and English Translation of the Medicine Buddha Service of the Liberation Rite of Water and Land at Fo Guang Shan Monastery*. A-R Editions, 2020. Middleton WI 53562. Full score + CD.

Evison, Gillian. 'Indian death rituals: The enactment of ambivalence'. D.Phil. thesis, Oxford University, 1989.

Fo Guang Shan, *20th Yearbook, 1987*, edited by the Religious Affairs Committee, headed by Shi Xin Ping. Gaoxiong: Fo Guang Shan, 1987.

Fu, Zhi Yin. *Chuan Din: Biography of Hsing Yun*. Taipei: Tian-Xia, 2nd ed., 1996.

Gildow, Douglas. 'The Chinese Buddhist ritual field: Common public rituals in PRC monasteries today'. *Journal of Chinese Buddhist Studies* 27 (2014): 59–127.

Gombrich, Richard F. *Precept and Practice*. Oxford: Clarendon Press, 1971.

Gombrich, Richard. *What the Buddha Thought*. Sheffield: Equinox, 2009.

Gombrich, Richard. 'Ambiguity and ambivalence in Buddhist treatment of the dead'. *Buddhist Studies Review* 35.1–2 (2018): 97–110.

Gombrich, Richard. 'Max Weber's work and the study of Buddhism today'. *Max Weber Studies* 18.1 (January 2018): 1–21.

Gombrich, Richard and Yu-Shuang Yao. 'A radical Buddhism for modern Confucians: Tzu Chi in socio-historical perspective'. *Buddhist Studies Review* 30.2 (November 2013): 237–59. https://doi.org/10.1558/bsrv.v30i2.237

Heinemann, Robert K. 'This world and the other power', in Heinz Bechert and Richard Gombrich (eds.), *The World of Buddhism*. London: Thames and Hudson, 1984: 212–30.

Hsing Yun, Ven. *Awakening*, 1 October 1961, reprinted as 'Everybody rich' (*Da jia fa cia*) in Ven Hsing Yun, *Writings in Awakening*, Collection on Buddhism 6. Gaoxiong: Fo Guang Publications, 1982: 48–50.

Hsing Yun. *The Biography of Sakyamuni Buddha*, trans. Alex Wong. Los Angeles: Buddha's Light Publishing, 2013 [Chinese ed. 1955–58].

Kane, P.V. *History of Dharmaśāstra* IV. Poona: Bhandarkar Oriental Research Institute, 1953.

Law, B.C. *The Buddhist Conception of Spirits*. London: Luzac, 1936.

Levine, Sarah and David N. Gellner. *Rebuilding Buddhism: The Theravada Movement in Twentieth-Century Nepal*. Cambridge, MA and London: Harvard University Press, 2005.

Madsen, Richard. *Democracy's Dharma: Religious Renaissance and Political Development in Taiwan*. Berkeley: University of California Press, 2007.

Madsen, Richard. 'Practice not dogma: Tzu-chi and the Buddhist tradition'. *Journal of the Oxford Centre for Buddhist Studies* 16 (May 2019): 87–97.

Malalgoda, Kitsiri. *Buddhism in Sinhalese Society 1750-1900*. Berkeley: University of California Press, 1976. https://doi.org/10.1525/9780520324466

Obeyesekere, Gananath. *Imagining Karma: Ethical Transformation in Amerindian, Buddhist, and Greek Rebirth*. Berkeley: University of California Press, 2002. https://doi.org/10.1525/california/9780520232204.001.0001

Pan Xuan and Ven. Hsing Yun. *Buddha Land in the Human World: The Making of the Buddha Memorial Center*, trans. Robert Smitheram, ed. Fo Guang Shan International Translation Center. Hacienda Heights, CA: Buddha's Light Publishing, 2013.

Reinke, Jen. 'Sacred secularities: Ritual and social engagement in a global Buddhist China'. *Religions*, 31 October 2018: 1–12.

Seaford, Richard. *Money and the Early Greek Mind*. Cambridge: Cambridge University Press, 2004. https://doi.org/10.1017/CBO9780511483080

Tarocco, Francesca. *The Cultural Practices of Modern Chinese Buddhism: Attuning the Dharma*. London and New York: Routledge, 2007.

Vasubandhu. *Abhidharmakośabhāṣya*, Vol. 1, translated into French by Louis de La Vallée Poussin, English translation by Leo M. Pruden. Berkeley, CA: Asian Humanities Press, 1991.

Welch, Holmes. *The Practice of Chinese Buddhism 1900-1950*. Cambridge, MA: Harvard University Press, 1967.

Xing, Ven. Ben. 'Nurturing the roots of Chinese Buddhism in Africa', https://www.buddhistdoor.net/featuresl/nurturing-the-roots-of-chinese-buddhism-in-africa, 29 December 2016.

Xinran. *China Witness*. London: Chatto and Windus, 2008.

Yao, Yu-Shuang. *Taiwan's Tzu Chi as Engaged Buddhism*. Leiden and Boston: Global Oriental, 2012. https://doi.org/10.1163/9789004231320

Yao, Yu-Shuang. 'Japanese influence on Buddhism in Taiwan'. *Journal of the Oxford Centre for Buddhist Studies* 6 (2014): 141–56.

Yao, Yu-Shuang and Richard Gombrich. 'Christianity as model and analogue in the formation of the "Humanistic" Buddhism of Tài Xū and Hsīng Yún'. *Buddhist Studies Review* 34.2 (2017): 205–237. https://doi.org/10.1558/bsrv.35392

Yao, Yu-Shuang and Richard Gombrich. 'Fo Guang Shan seen through telescope and microscope'. *Journal of the Oxford Centre for Buddhist Studies* 14 (2018): 128–55.

INDEX

Page numbers in *italics* refer to illustrations.
Lower case *italic n* after page number refers to footnote.

Abhidharmakośabhāṣya (Vasubandhu) 51–52, 59
Africa
    Amitofo Care Centre (ACC) 117–19
    Buddhism in 108, 119–20
Amida (Sanskrit: Amitābha) Buddha 14–15, 21–22
Amidism (*also* Pure Land Buddhism) 14–15, 20–26, 88–89, 105, 110–11
Amitofo Care Centres (ACC) 117–19
ancestor worship 26, 38, 49–50, 99
arts (Buddhist) 29, 55, 64, 111
asceticism 16, 18–21, 90
Asoka, Emperor 44, 96
'Assembly of lay disciples' 91
Awakening (Fo Guang Shan journal) 65

Bhagavad Gītā 13
Bhaiṣajyaguru (Medicine Buddha) 85, 86n5, 88, 103 *see also* Obon; Water and Land rituals
bhikkhuni *see* nuns
BLIA *see* Buddha Light International Association, the
bodhisattva 10, 35, 49
    compassion 55–56
    Kṣitigarbha 85
    precepts 86
    serving all beings 20, 98–99
    worship of 64, 84, 102
Brahmajāla Sūtra 74
Brahminism (*also* Brahminical Hinduism) 38, 40–41, 43–45, 48, 50, 97
Buddha Light International Association, the (BLIA) 5, 69, 75, 77, 77, 112
Buddha Memorial Center (BMC) 110–14
Buddha's tooth relic 112–13

'Buddhism for human life' 6, 54–56, 62–63
    see also 'Humanistic Buddhism'

capitalism 27–28
Catholicism 4, 76–77, 120
Chan (*also* Ch'an; Zen)
    Buddhism 14–15, 105
    hall 15, 20, 89, 96
    meditation 15, 73
    monasteries 15
    practice 20, 57, 102
chanting
    and American gospel preachers 26
    'Assisting dying' 106
    Fo Guang Shan ceremonies and performances 84–86, 88–89, 91, 102–104, 109
    Fo Guang Shan training for monastics 73
    funeral rituals 105–107
    Hsing Yun's radio broadcasts 65
    society 65, 71
Cheng Yen, Master 55–56, 62–63
Chiang Kai Shek *see* Jiang Jie Shi
Christianity 60
    features of 7–9, 27
    influence on Fo Guang Shan 4, 24n19, 26–27, 64, 76–77, 103, 109
    and Tai Xu 4, 37, 70
Confucianism 8, 12, 60, 76–77

Dharma (*also* Dhamma; 'teachings of the Buddha') 53, 71, 84, 89, 104, 112, 119–20
dharma (constituent of reality) 20, 27, 64, 70, 87–88, 108
Dharma Drum 6, 27, 54
Dharma Seal 116
Dharmaguptaka *Vinaya* 73
dukkha 3, 16–17, 47

'engaged Buddhism' *see* 'Humanistic Buddhism'

Enlightenment (*nibbāna* in Pali) 10, 17, 19, 55
   Buddha's 18, 85*n*3
   of Kuan Yin 84
   nirvana 23, 37, 39, 42, 47
   by one's own efforts (*jiriki*) 14
   through the help of a Buddha (*tariki*) 14–15, 22
   see also nirvana
eschatology 19, 24
'ethicizing' 40, 42
ethics
   and ancestral worship 38
   in the Buddha's teaching 34, 41, 95
   Confucian 56
   Hsing Yun on 24
   and karma 39, 41–42
   Tai Xu on 20

fahui 84–86
Feeding the Hungry Ghosts *see* Water and Land rituals
filial piety 50, 85, 87, 101, 105–106
Fo Guang University 7, 30, 74–75
funeral
   Hsing Yun views on 37, 102, 106–107
   rituals 38, 102, 105–106
   Tai Xu's views on 20, 37, 105
   see also mortuary rituals

gender roles in Fo Guang Shan administration 33, 56, 72–73
gods 9–10, 24, 42, 47–49, 84, 98–99
Great Compassion
   Mantra 84, 108
   ritual 37, 86–88, 87, 98, 103
   see also Bhaiṣajyaguru; Water and Land rituals
Great Repentance of the Emperor Liang 86*n*5 *see also* Water and Land rituals

Han and Tibetan cultural association 90, 112
heaven(s)
   Christianity and 27
   Gananath Obeyeskere on 40, 47–48
   populated by gods in Theravāda Buddhism 47–48
   Pure Land imagined as 23–24, 66, 111
   rebirth in 9, 15–16, 22, 37–38, 40–41, 43
hierarchy
   of authority (Taiwan) 76
   Buddhist temple 32–33
   clerical 31, 56
   Fo Guang Shan 56, 76–77
   in Hinduism 8
Hinduism 8–9, 14, 42
   Brahminical 38, 40–41, 43–45, 48, 50, 97
   gods 9, 96

   temple 96
'Humanistic Buddhism' ('engaged Buddhism') 110
   College of 110
   Dharma Drum 6, 54
   Fo Guang Shan 6, 23–25, 26–27, 54–56, 61–63, 112–13
   Hui Li 119
   Tai Xu (Taixu) 6, 26, 61–62
   Tzu Chi 6, 54–56, 62–63
Hsing Yun (HY), Most Venerable Master *xii*, *72*, *120*
   American influence 26, 29, 32
   attitude to wealth 21, 27–28, 57, 63
   early life 6, 30, 57–61, 71
   enjoyment of life 3–4, 19, 21, 26, 29–30, 63–64
   on funerary rituals 37, 106–107
   and politics 31
   pragmatism 20–21, 33–36, 100, 111
   proselytizing activities 61, 64–69, 71
   and Pure Land tradition 21, 23–26
   as religious leader 19–20, 55, 57, 76–77, 111
   and secular education 30, 71–75
   treatment of women 33–34
Hui Li, Venerable Master 117–20, *210*
Huiye, Venerable 117
'Humanistic Buddhism' (*also* 'engaged Buddhism'; *renjian* Buddhism) 6, 23–27, 54, 61–62, 110, 112–13, 119

individualism 9, 23, 34, 39, 55, 103, 109
   against the collective 53, 62–63, 96–99
   and Confucianism 76
intention
   ethics and 95
   internal 23, 57
   karma 34–35, 39–42, 44–45, 49, 51–52, 98
   merit and 44–45, 49, 97–98
   rituals with the right 100–101

Jain 8, 16, 18–19, 21, 38, 40–41
Jiang Jie Shi (Chiang Kai Shek), General 6, 26, 60, 71, 89–90
jiriki ('own power') 14
John Paul II, Pope 77

kamma *see* karma
karma (kamma) 10
   in Brahminism/Hinduism 38, 45, 97
   in the Buddha's teaching 34–35, 38–45, 49
   collective 39*n*5, 50–53, 96–98
   expunging bad 41, 45, 97
   in Jainism 38
   Mahāyāna view 39*n*5, 49

and (mortuary) rituals 87, 97–98, 102, 106–107
    Theravādin view 47, 63
    -vipāka (pay-off) 40
Khuddaka Nikāya 43
Kṣitigarbha 85
Kuomintang (KMT) 60, 71

laity, the 5, 62, 102, 115
    'Assisted dying' chanting by 106
    Bodhisattva precepts for 86
    Buddha's teaching to 34
    Buddhist Light International Association (BLIA) for 5, 69, 75
    Fo Guang Shan and 64–69, 72–74, 77, 91, 104
    Theravāda tradition 96
Lei Yin temple 65, 71
Ling Jiu Mountain monastery 115–16

Majjhima Nikāya 18n5, 46
Mahāvīra ('Great Hero'), founder of Jainism 16
Mahāyāna Buddhism 6, 10–12, 14, 17, 116
    Brahmajāla Sūtra 74
    'Humanistic Buddhism' 62–63, 119
    idea of transferable merit 49, 98–99
    Nanhua temple in Johannesburg (South Africa) 118
Malawi 117–19
mataka dānēs (Sinhala) 46
Medicine Buddha (Bhaiṣajyaguru ceremony) 85, 86n5, 88, 103
meditation 46, 58, 100, 116, 119
    Chan (hall) 15, 20, 89, 96
    at Fo Guang Shan 20, 24, 55, 73, 109
    and self-control 17, 19
    as individual activity 96–97
    Tai Xi on 20
merit
    transfer of 41–42, 44–50, 85–89, 97–98, 101
    and rituals for the dead 85, 98–99, 105–107
'Middle Way' 18–19, 21, 28
monasteries, Buddhist
    Chinese 15, 76, 99, 101–102
    Fo Guang Shan 59, 72, 76, 84–86, 88–91
    full ordination at 74
    income generated by 96, 100–102
    Myanmar 116
    seminars and universities founded by 72–73, 75
    Taiwanese 72, 75, 100
monasticism, Buddhist 49, 96, 99
money
    Fo Guang Shan and making 63, 71, 90–91, 100, 102, 106, 114

Index 125

    handling and use of money 28, 34–35, 106
    as metaphor for merit 45–46, 98
    see also wealth
monotheism 9–10, 29
morality
    and Fo Guang Shan 55, 57
    and karma 34, 97
    and path to Enlightenment 17
    and rituals 87, 95
    and self-control 19, 39–42, 44
mortuary rituals 6, 27, 37–38, 43–46, 95–99, 101–102, 105–107 see also ancestor worship
music 111
    Hsing Yun and 29–30, 55, 64–66, 103
    rituals and 27, 103–104

Nanhai Buddhist Association 117
nirvana 23, 37, 39, 42, 47 see also Enlightenment
Noble Truths 3, 16–19
novice(s) 26, 72, 72, 73, 75, 116–17
nuns 18, 87, 115
    African Buddhist 118
    chanting 104–105
    and education 71–72, 74, 76
    Fo Guang Shan 33, 74, 76
    and handling money 28, 34–35
    Hsing Yun and ordaining 32
    and 'Humanistic Buddhism' 62
    Mahāvīra's celibate order for 16
    and political activism 31
    Roman Catholic 77
    Theravāda 32, 112
    Tibetan 32

Obeyesekere, Gananath 40, 47
Obon 37, 85, 86n5, 102–103 see also Bhaiṣajyaguru; Great Compassion; Water and Land rituals
ordination
    bestowed by Hsing Yun 32, 118
    Bodh Gaya international Full 112
    education as prerequisite for 70
    Fo Guang Shan 73–74, 118
    śikṣamāṇā 73
    'triple platform' 73, 116
    see also tonsure
orthodoxy 7, 36
    Brahmin 44
orthopraxy 7, 36

Pali Canon 18, 21, 43, 49, 74n8
paradise ('the Western Paradise') 22, 25, 106
penances 41–42, 45, 97 see also repentance rituals; Water and Land rituals
peta (Pali) see preta

126 Index

Petavatthu (book of Khuddaka Nikāya) 43, 46
pilgrimage 53, 68, 68
politics 31, 57
polytheism 9–11, 49
poverty 27–28, 58, 60, 62, 76, 118
precepts 46, 59, 73, 112
    Arhat 116
    Bhikkuni 112
    Bodhisattva 86
    the five 86, 119
    full ordination 74, 112, 118
    in the Mahāyāna *Brahmajāla Sūtra* 74
    Yogācāra 74
preta (Sanskrit; *peta* in Pali; ghost) 43–44, 46, 48 see also *Petavatthu*
Protestantism 4, 109
Pure Land Buddhism (*also* Amidism) 14–15, 20–26, 88–89, 105, 110–11
purity 14, 23–25
Puxian Humanitarian Association 118

rebirth (cycle of) 95, 106
    and believers in the Pure Land 14, 22–23
    escape from 3, 9, 15–17, 37, 39–44, 46–47
    and filial piety 49–50, 101
    and Fo Guang Shan 23–25
    mantra associated with 107–108
    and worshippers of Amida 22
renjian Buddhism see 'Humanistic Buddhism'; Tai Xu, 'Buddhism for Human Life'
repentance rituals 102–103, 105, 108 see also penances; Water and Land rituals
responsibility
    collective 50, 62
    individual 34, 38–39, 49, 53, 62, 96–97
rituals 7
    and ancestor worship 49–50
    Asoka on 44, 95–96
    the Buddha on 41, 43–44, 95
    of Dharmaguptaka *Vinaya* 73
    fahui (Dharma assembly) 84, 86
    Fo Guang Shan 26–27, 61, 69, 84–91, 98, 102–109
    the Great Compassion 37, 86–87, 87, 88, 98, 103
    mortuary 6, 27, 37–38, 43–46, 95–99, 101–102, 105–107
    in the People's Republic of China (PRC) 99–100
    repentance 102–103, 105, 108
    role of music in 27, 103–104
    Sangha and the preservation and cultivation of 12, 96, 99
    Water and Land 87, 87, 88, 98, 103, 117

'Water and Land ceremony of universal *paccaya*' 37, 86–87, 87, 88, 98, 103
Roman Catholicism 4, 76–77, 119–20

'salvation' 9–10, 40, 119 see also Enlightenment; rebirth (cycle of), escape from
Saṅgha (the ordained) 5, 13, 16, 29
    Buddha's framework of the 34
    centrality of performing rituals for the dead 96, 99, 101–102
    educational reform of 30, 70, 75–76
    of FSG 30–33, 55–57, 59, 75–77, 104–105
    mataka dānēs 46
    and the preservation and cultivation of texts and rituals 12
    property ownership and wealth of the 27–28, 33
    schism within 115
    Theravāda tradition 96, 112
self-control 17, 19, 95–96
Sheng Yen, Venerable Master 27–28, 54
Shinran 21–22, 24
sīla 95 see also morality
soteriology 14–16, 25, 40, 48
South Africa 108, 118–19
Sūtra
    Amitābha 58, 107
    Avataṃsaka 82, 84
    Bhaiṣajyaguru (Medicine Buddha) 85, 86n5, 88, 91
    Brahmajāla 74
    Diamond 58
    of Great Compassion 84, 108
    of the Sixth Patriarch 66, 92, 118
    of Water and Land 88

Tai Xu (*also* Taixu), Master
    'Buddhism for Human Life' 6, 20, 26, 61–62, 96, 105, 107–109
    criticized preoccupation with rituals for the dead 6, 11, 17–18, 20, 26, 37, 96, 101–102
    (monastic) education 30, 62, 70, 75–76
    Hsing Yun's teacher 2, 6, 21, 32, 60–61, 71
    reactions to Christianity 4, 24n19, 37, 103
    see also 'Humanistic Buddhism'
Taoism 8, 12–13
tariki ('other power') 14, 22
technology, modern 26, 62, 64, 66, 108
Theravāda ('the teaching of the elders')
    conservative tradition 10, 50, 62–64, 99, 119
    gods in the heavens 47

monastery 96–97
nuns 32, 112
ordination 73, 116
Thich Nhat Hạnh 6, 109
Three Refuges 66, 84–85, 91, 107
Tibet, Buddhism 71, 80, 82, 90
    Kunga Dorje Rinpoche, Lama 112–13
    see also Han and Tibetan cultural association
tonsure ceremony 72, 73–74, 91
    of Hsing Yun 58
    of Hui Li 118
    of Xin Dao 116
    see also ordination
transfer of merit see merit, transfer of
Tripiṭaka 65, 67
Tzu Chi 3, 6, 54–56, 62–63

United States of America (USA)
    capitalism 27
    influence of American culture on Fo Guang Shan 25–27, 29, 32, 68
    radio broadcast on Buddhist teaching and Chinese culture in 65–66
    Xi Lai Temple (California) 26, 32, 88, 90, 108–109
Universal Gate (Buddhist magazine) 65
Upaniṣads 40

Vasubandhu, Abhidharmakośabhāṣya 51–52, 59
vegetarianism 58, 68, 84, 114–15, 118
Vimāna-vatthu (book of Khaddaka Nikāya) 43
Vinaya 34, 112
    Dharmaguptaka 73
vipāka ('maturation') 40, 52–53
Virgin Mary 2, 9, 68
vows 10, 20, 86, 95
    of Hsing Yun 59

of Hui Li 118
of Xin Ping 89

Water and Land rituals
    Great Repentance of the Emperor Liang 86n5
    Nanhai Buddhist Association 117
    'Ritual of Water and Land ceremony of universal paccaya' 37, 86–87, 87, 88, 98, 103
    and Sky Service 117
    see also Bhaiṣajyaguru; Great Compassion; Obon
wealth
    the Buddha and 17
    Christianity and 9, 27
    Hsing Yun's views on 21, 27–28, 57, 63
    merit associated with the Great Compassion Mantra 108
Weber, Max 4–5, 16
'Western Paradise' 22, 106
women's role in Fo Guang Shan 33, 56, 72–73
World Fellowship of Buddhists 110, 112–13

Xi Lai (also Xilai) (California)
    radio broadcast from 65–66
    temple 26, 32, 88, 90, 108–109
    speech of Hsing Yun at the University of 106
Xin Ping, Venerable 89–90
Xin Dao, Venerable (also Hsintao) 115–17
Xingyun see Hsing Yun

Yin Shun, Venerable 10
Yogācāra 59, 74
Yuanjui Educational Fund 118

Zen see Chan

www.ingramcontent.com/pod-product-compliance
Lightning Source LLC
Chambersburg PA
CBHW050929240426
43671CB00019B/2963